COPING WITH CRISIS

COPING
WITH
CRISIS

SARAH MORRIS

Chicago Review Press

First Edition
First Printing 1978

ISBN (clothbound edition) 0-914090-41-0
ISBN (paperback edition) 0-914090-42-9
Library of Congress Catalog Number 77-93720

Book design and typography by Claire J. Mahoney

Published by
Chicago Review Press, Inc.
215 West Ohio Street
Chicago, Illinois 60610

Contents

Surviving Personal Crisis

A young wife and mother gradually but steadily losing her eyesight . . . A middle-aged woman unable to think, to function, sorrowing because her husband of twenty apparently happy years asked for a divorce . . . A highly trained scientist with a family to support, released from his job in an economy move, competing for work in a market where there are no openings for his skills . . . A high school boy learning to live in a wheelchair after an automobile accident . . . The founder and president of a big manufacturing firm floundering in his retirement . . . A mother and a father grieving over the disappearance of their daughter, a run-away . . . A doctor battling to cure

7

his alcoholic wife . . . A mother and father watching their ten-year-old son die of leukemia.

The examples are typical of the personal crises that thousands of people must meet and learn to cope with every day. The purpose of this book is to examine the effects of such tragedies — the invariable "shocks that flesh is heir to", as Shakespeare put it, in a way that will enable men and women to go on functioning and eventually overcome them.

Anyone who has faced a crisis knows the emotional paralysis and fear that can grip you and prevent you from being able to cope with normal living. You may wonder temporarily if you can survive the tragedy and still remain a whole person. Being completely out of control is a helpless and terrifying experience. But there is hardly anyone alive who has not experienced such a period of trial.

People in crisis are suffering the most painful emotions that a human being can experience. Their inner struggle may seem to threaten their sanity. However, they need to face the reality of what has happened. Then gradually each must learn to accept his individual crisis so that eventually he can continue to live a life in which there is honest satisfaction. An eventual adjustment must be made, unlikely as it may seem when grief is fresh.

Yet studies show that there is too little recognition by others of what crises cost those who are suffering them. People in our country find it hard to acknowledge deep trouble in the lives of others. There is a tendency to respond awkwardly because they are not practiced in ways of showing compassion. Trouble is not part of the American dream. We are used to responding to success, health, beauty, and plenty. It is a grave shortcoming of our society that too few people truly understand what someone in a crisis goes through. People in trouble should not feel hurt by the distant and awkward discomfort of friends who try to show their concern. A few may even mistakenly suggest that getting back to life as usual as soon as possible is the surest way of finding a way through tragedy.

This lack of general understanding of the ways to cope with a crisis makes it very hard for people who enter the lonely and unfamiliar world of grief. For grief it is, although we usually think of grief only in connection with mourning someone who has died. They know little about how to deal with their own bewildering feelings and have even less understanding of how to handle some of the attitudes of others.

However, most people find support in an almost miraculous emotional strength that gradually develops with those who must work their way through a crisis situation. According to a well-known psychologist, Rollo May, "You'll find this unexpected strength because there are unused capacities which you will begin to discover."

Elizabeth, a quite remarkable person, exemplifies the power of this kind of growth. She is an attractive woman, about thirty years old, who walks with the help of braces and crutches.

She said, "I was divorced and right after that I had an accident — one that paralyzed me permanently. I will always have to use these braces and these crutches. I have an eight-year-old son, a little fellow anyone would be proud of. I surely am. His father's stopped sending child support money, and it's hard to manage on just my disability check. But I can't earn anything at all or I'd lose that check, and I certainly can't let that happen."

Then she shifted to talking about her feelings. "You know, I've grown so much in the last three years that I've had to cope with learning to be crippled. Somehow I'm a stronger person; I'm better able to manage my life and the problems that have to be solved. If I had to choose between my handicap and being the person I used to be, I'd take my handicap any time. Adjusting to this", and she glanced down at her legs, "has meant everything to me. That accident changed my life all right — and for the better. Before I guess I was crippled on the inside, and now I'm just crippled on the outside. So in a funny kind of way the accident helped me. I never felt so alive and — well on top of things as I do now!"

That's Elizabeth's testimony to the emotional growth which she paid for at such a cost to herself — an almost unbelievable gratitude for the intangible dividend of greater inner strength which she recognized as an asset she can depend on for the rest of her life.

I have walked every step of the road that people in crisis follow. I walked it when my husband died. My feelings were so confused at the time that I was not sure I would ever be myself again. Having studied psychology, I turned to it for answers. I searched almost desperately to discover ideas that would help me understand my new and frightening feelings so that I could find a way to cope with them.

As I began to put into practice what I had found, I gradually improved. There was nothing sudden or dramatic about my change, but instead of feeling that I was floating helplessly, I began to feel that I had some sense of direction.

The principles and approaches that were helpful to me apply to managing many kinds of crises: those caused by normal life changes as well as tragic ones such as divorce, physical handicaps, loss of a job, unspoken realization of life failure, tragedy that comes to a loved one, and finally that caused by the death of someone loved.

There are many things that can happen which bring tragedy into life, and some very personal tragedies may not be specifically mentioned here. However, the basic ideas developed in this book can be adapted to learning something about how to deal with almost any individual crisis.

Fortunately there are resources available to help people in crisis. Of course those resources vary according to each person and each problem. But some are basic.

Faith is of first importance as a resource. People with deep personal faith accept and resolve the grief of a crisis more quickly and easily than those who do not have such faith. This is because the tragic experience can be understood in the light of a whole framework of supporting beliefs, rather than approached as one that stands alone as a single event unrelated to established and important life values. However, beliefs vary so that they cannot be discussed specifically. The very best resource for each individual is someone who shares his faith, someone who can help interpret his personal crisis in the light of their common beliefs.

Such a person may be a part of the second resource — people who stand by, who are there to talk with, to cry with during the weeks and months of learning to live through and finally beyond the crisis that at first seemed too much to bear. There are, of course, not many people who are willing to walk this road with others. But each person in trouble needs only one or two friends who understand and accept whatever thoughts and feelings and behavior someone in crisis experiences.

There is a last and most important resource. Some people cannot make progress in meeting a major crisis; they are just as confused and upset a year or so after the crisis as they were soon after it happened. This is not unusual. They find they need help in handling their emotional problems just as they need help from a doctor in handling their physical ones. Such people should see a counselor.

However, the difficulty in going to a counselor is that most people are not used to consulting one. We hesitate to go to a counselor because we don't want to think there's "something wrong." But the truth is that there may be something wrong emotionally, just as there may be something wrong physically if a headache is the symptom. Everyone hopes that he never has a crisis greater than he can cope with. But there are some problems so great that nearly all of us would need help. So when people reach their individual breaking points, they should go to a specialist in understanding people's emotions.

The best counselor for you may be one a friend you

know has gone to or knows about. Or perhaps your doctor or minister may be able to help you find one. Often there are personal counselors as part of a church staff. Another very good source is the local mental health organization. Such organizations usually charge according to ability to pay. One important point to keep in mind when seeking a counselor is that you should feel confidence in whomever you visit, and you may not find that special person until you have gone to see several.

This is a great deal to say about counselors, but they represent a resource we don't use often and so few people are familiar with when to use them or where to find them. Some people not only need to consult a counselor — they want to because their lives are so unhappy that they don't want to waste another day going through the motions of living with the sick, tight feeling that seems to paralyze them. They want to learn how they can truly live again.

There are some fortunate people who "take life in stride" and seem able to handle whatever comes their way. A remarkable grandmother is one such person. She had been blinded at eighteen when her only child was a baby. Soon after, her husband died. Much later she was engaged to be married, but the man she expected to marry was killed in a freak accident. Despite all this tragedy she was able to say: "I have known many kinds of sorrows, some brought on by my own wilfullness, others by outside forces, but I have always found, without exception, that if I did the best I could, weak and faltering as that best sometimes was, that eventually, perhaps not soon, but eventually, it all led to a richer, deeper, experience than

I could possibly have known without the pain. I believe that. And many a time it has been my solace and my strength for the way which seemed so hard."

People can grow to meet crises in life. However, in doing this they are forced to discover new capacities and strengths within themselves they did not know they had. You too can be one of these.

Usual Life Changes

There are many usual life changes that come to all of us. They are a part of our lives from babyhood on.

In a church nursery where children stayed while their parents were in church, a dozen two- and three-year-olds were contentedly playing at the far end of the room, but one little girl was in a paroxysm of anger. She threw herself against the door leading to the hall, beating on it and screaming. She had been confronted with an adjustment she was having more than usual difficulty making!

We all experience tension as we go through the ordinary growth periods in life — being left with someone other than mother for the first time, going to the first day of school alone, going off to work or to college as a teen-ager, marrying, and retiring. These represent some of the typical adjustments. The stronger your sense of self the more easily you will adjust your self-image to each new role. *And the better you are able to make ordinary adjust-ments, the better you will be able to deal with tragic ones should they come to you, for you will have had successful practice in dealing with change.*

To venture into new experiences quite naturally causes tension, but not to venture means losing an opportunity to grow. As an individual ventures and so masters a new as-pect of his life, he is strengthening his sense of self, his most important weapon, which is indispensable in getting through a lifetime of change.

There are recognized principles for dealing with these ordinary changes that can be *anticipated in a lifetime.*

SUCH CHANGES CAN BE PLANNED FOR.

Adjustment is not so difficult, if you have become familiar with the change that is coming to you. A child going to school for the first time may need to walk past the school several times if he is not familiar with it, and then he may want to go in and visit and meet the teacher. To avoid having children make too abrupt an adjustment from home to school, mothers may take their children to school the first day and stay to watch them play. Perhaps the mothers even pass crayons or answer children's questions and so naturally become a part of the schoolroom situation before they leave to go home. Orientation sessions at businesses and schools, premarital discussion groups, and prenatal classes for parents are all performing the same psychological service of preparation. A doctor usually discusses an operation with a patient so he will know what to expect in his care and not fear the unfamiliar routines.

One group of people who need to plan ahead are mothers whose children are soon to leave home at adolescence, for such women can become empty-handed and empty-hearted. Each needs to plan for this change and become gradually involved in other interests in the years before the children leave home. Some may work — either full- or part-time, some may return to school, others may do more church work, join a club, or take a recreation class in exercise, weaving, dancing or photography. The possibilities are endless.

After one woman's children left home, she did more housework. She changed the bed linen daily; each week she waxed the parquet floor in the hall, rubbing alternate squares in different directions. She made more cakes and canned more peas. She was filling her time, however, by doing more of the things she was familiar with rather than venturing or trying something different. Perhaps this intensified household activity satisfied her own individual demands. Some women play bridge harder, adorn themselves with increasing concentration or make a career of endless shopping. The test of how useful such activities are lies in whether or not doing them makes each woman a happy and fulfilled person.

Also people who retire must surely know when they are nearing their retirement age. They usually need to plan ahead in order to fill their time and perhaps their pocketbooks. The time to do this planning is months or even years before actual retirement. A teacher knew he must retire when he was sixty-five. In the six months before retirement he was frantically busy. He was not only carrying on his regular work but he was also applying for work in schools across the country. This required a huge correspondence and some trips for interviews. In case he did not find a new job, he was also allowing himself to be drawn into community activities that he had never dared take time for before, and he even became interested in doing some writing. Although he enjoyed his work, he did not dread retiring because he had so much to look forward to that used his abilities to capacity.

Not all people want or need much activity after retirement. Each of us is different in what we require at any stage of life. We each need enough activity to enrich life but not so much that we are overwhelmed nor so little that we lie fallow. Some people have been fortunate enough to work out a life with just the right amount of activity in it. It has even been suggested that the search for this optimum may be what the pursuit of happiness is about. Rather than depend on events which come his way, an independent person who feels he needs more stimulation seeks out new experience and new risk within the limits he can tolerate. Such a person may do as little as to go away for a weekend alone or make a new friend. Or he may take off and go around the world.

When a dynamic and brilliant industrial executive retired at seventy-two, he fulfilled a life dream, and that was to have a business of his own. He built a small plant, manufactured a product he had invented, and marketed it. Later he sold the business at a profit and was retained as a consultant.

Another man, a surgeon, retired at sixty-five because he did not want to continue to operate as he slowly lost his manual dexterity. Then, unexpectedly, he was asked to enter a whole new field of medicine, public health, which he had to study as a beginner. He became the Director of Public Health for the community he had served all his life as a doctor. In the seven years before his death, he built a health department that rose from one of the poorest to one of the highest ratings in the country according to national evaluations.

These two men built second careers after they retired and each was satisfied according to his own needs. However, some people would not want to take as much steady responsibility as these two assumed. Many people do not feel a need for greater stimulation and do not want to add risk and responsibilities to their lives. They may fish, golf, take trips, garden — doing full-time things they had done part-time in their busy lives.

A Christmas letter that came to me several years ago showed the natural acceptance of growing older by a remarkably vigorous and brilliant engineer. On retirement he had not planned new activities so much as he had developed a philosophy which absorbed change.

How distressing it is to talk with someone who cannot adjust to the fact that life's shadows are stretching toward the east, irrevocably and without pity, that here and there our human machinery tends to wear out and whose general attitude toward the future is so well expressed in the following dismal words:

> *My days are in the yellow leaf,*
> *The flowers and fruits of love are gone,*
> *The worm, the canker and the grief —*
> *Are mine alone.*

How jubilant one feels when a comparably aged person smiles and tersely says:

> *Grow old along with me,*
> *The best is yet to be.*

One of the best assets of getting old is that many of the things you craved and couldn't have when you were young — you no longer want.

CHANGE SHOULD BE BALANCED WITH THE FAMILIAR.

The teacher who planned for his retirement was putting into use another principle that makes change less difficult. He was planning for change while his life was still stable.

He began his new activities while he was involved with the old. There was no sharp break between the two.

A man put this principle to work in his active life as a salesman. He felt that he needed to keep a sense of security in his life as he traveled from one country to another. To do this he kept, as best he could, a stable daily routine of exercise, rest, and study, quite independent of the demands made on him by his business responsibilities in different parts of the world.

Sometimes stability is found in a relationship — one that is reliable and steady and always there. Wives and husbands often fill this need for each other. Young children quite naturally illustrate this principle. A child will play for a while and then return to his mother to renew his confidence by sitting on her lap or telling her something important. And when satisfied, he will leave and go play again.

THE CAPACITY TO ADAPT TO CHANGE SHOULD NOT BE OVERBURDENED.

Although there is a reserve of adaptive energy in all of us, it is wise not to overload our systems. A young woman whose husband got a new job had to move from New York City to San Diego. Although they looked forward to the move, they were facing a major change. It is believed that in adjusting to such a change the whole adaptive system is making major neural and hormonal adjustments. In addition, unfortunately, she had to have an operation a few weeks before the move. She was seriously overburdening her adaptive system, having to go through moving before she had fully regained her strength after the shock of the operation. She was weary and almost depressed by the overwhelming number of decisions she had to make as she dragged through the move. This overburdening of her adaptive system could not have been avoided. But, when possible, do not plan more normal wear and tear from change than you can easily manage.

Dr. Thomas H. Holmes of Seattle, Washington, has found that the more an individual experiences change in life, the more likely he is to get sick. Dr. Holmes has devised a point system for rating the relative impact on health for forty-three different life changes. Joyful changes, including marriage, vacations and outstanding personal achievement, can be stressful and hazardous to health as well as tragic changes such as bereavement, divorce, and going to jail. Dr. Holmes feels that too much change experienced too quickly overworks the imperfect adaptive system, lowers bodily resistance, and boosts the probability of sickness.

An electrical circuit that is overburdened blows a fuse. People who overburden their adaptive systems also give in to pressure. They too "blow a fuse." Some people may show this physically as weariness or even in an actual illness, such as a cold. Or they may show it emotionally in irritability, or women — and some men — may show it by crying.

EVERY PERSON HAS TO TRY TO FIND HIS OWN BALANCE OF QUIET AND ACTIVITY, OR SECURITY AND ADVENTURE IN LIFE.

Some people may not demand enough of themselves. They may be bored and restless and witness to their own failure to grow. They have been tempted to allow their lives to stagnate because life made too few demands on them, and they made no new demands on themselves. They allowed themselves to get by with the same emotional maturity, the same values, the same interests and friends that served them well at a previous stage. On the other hand others find themselves frayed with too much change and activity.

The measure of a good life is in whether it feeds the individual. An outwardly quiet life may be one of deep contentment or it may be one frustrated with gray monotony. An active life may be one of real challenge or it may be one dissipated in frantic busyness. If you have made a practice of seeking your own individual best balance, you will carry this habit into the various stages of change in your life. You add or drop extra activities as the core of your life changes in its demands on you. The object always is to find the special combination which makes life good to live for you as an individual.

Your Own
Tragic Life Changes

Perhaps up to now you have had rather superficial experience with crises and so, in experiencing tragedy, you may be entering a world that is not familiar to you. People acknowledge tragedy in others' lives with an ordinary but sincere gesture such as a card, flowers, or a note saying, "I am thinking of you." But the day-to-day, long-term impact of tragedy on individual lives is seldom fully realized by others. So in coping with your own problem, you probably have little basis for knowing how people feel or act in experiencing a major life change.

A first natural reaction to crisis is usually one of disbelief, numbness and shock, not knowing where to turn,

a lost feeling, or even denial. Sometimes a surface acceptance serves to protect you for a while; but this cannot
be maintained for long. There is no way to anticipate
the time and intensity or exact form of your first response
to personal crisis.

After the first unguarded reaction to your problem, you
must learn to face the fact of what has happened to you.
This is a long, slow experience that cannot have a time
limit placed on it nor need there be one, but it can be
broken down in several aspects.

FIRST . . .

The hurt, the grief, the painful part of this whole experience is facing it mentally. This you do in every way open
to you.

1. Of course there is no way you can help but *think* about
it. At first thinking is constant; it consumes every waking
moment, crowding into every dimension of your mind.
Attempting to break the ties to the familiar and the supporting reality of the past becomes real torture. Breaking
the ties does not mean that you never think of your life
as it was. It simply means that eventually when you are
reminded of it, you will not be emotionally upset.

2. Then there are certain people you can *talk* to endlessly
about every aspect of the problem — the changes that
have come into your life and your fears for the future.

You may be able to talk to someone close to you who grieves with you. If so, you are fortunate. On the other hand, you may feel you want to spare those you love the depth of your first despair, although eventually when you are feeling less desperate, you will need to be open with them. The strange thing about finding people to talk to is that they are not always the ones you know well. It is often the *kind* of person that is important, and such people may even seek you out. Fortunately there are people in the world who have empathy for others and are drawn to those in trouble. They listen to us; they even despair and hope with us.

However, it is not always easy to find people who are sympathetic listeners. There are some people who do not seem to want to take the responsibility of being involved in trouble about which they think they can do nothing. In a study done in England by an anthropologist, he and his staff interviewed hundreds of people who were bereaved in order to discover people's attitude to those in grief. He discovered that "the majority . . . tend to treat mourning as morbid self-indulgence, and to give social admiration to the bereaved who hide their grief so fully that none would guess anything had happened." He reported that "mourning is treated as if it were a weakness . . . instead of a psychological necessity." Do not be surprised if you find people who reflect this attitude toward you and your tragedy.

The need to find people to talk to is considered so important that there is a trend now to follow the lead of Alcoholics Anonymous and programs for drug addicts.

Groups of people are formed who have experienced certain physical disabilities, who have been widowed, or who have lost a child. In these programs, a "care-giver", one who has suffered a specific problem, helps someone newly faced with it. If you do not have a group in your community which can meet your particular need, talk to someone who has had deep trouble of any kind, because that person knows what you are going through. However, all such people are not good "care-givers." You need to talk about your immediate and terrible problem. You do not, at this time, need to learn about another's.

It often helps if that person is as much like you as possible. In general a well-to-do older divorcee would not be of as great help to a young divorced mother as another woman who has the responsibility of little children and who is working in order to support her family. Likewise a crippled man assisted by an attendant, a car, and every known device to help him live a nearly normal life might not understand the problems of a poor boy confined to his hand-propelled wheelchair.

However, in the last analysis, it is the empathy and the long-time support such a person can give that are of first importance. It is the quality of the person, the caring of the person that matters. As a speaker said in a meeting on mourning in Holland, "What we can do, and indeed what I believe we have to do, is to be so alongside another person that by our very sharing with him, we enable him to bear what he must. A caring community makes a real contribution to someone in trouble."

You cannot tell how many weeks or months you will

need to talk to other people. But there will come a time when the need is less urgent and the talks will be less frequent.

3. One way of facing your problem mentally is to *write* about it. Keep a journal, write letters to close friends who are near enough to talk to, or just write down what you feel and think.

SECOND . . .

After you have allowed yourself to dwell on your problem *mentally,* there comes a blessed and welcome time when you unexpectedly begin to accept it *emotionally.* You know that when you force yourself to do something because you think you should, it is difficult. But when you do something because you *want* to, it is easier. You do the first for mental reasons. You do the second for emotional ones. The moment your emotions, not your mind, prompt you, you have turned the corner. Because such a change is an inner one, I must illustrate this important turning-point with an experience of my own. The change from mental to emotional motivation is so subtle and the balance between the two is such a delicate one that insight into another's dynamics would be difficult for me to assess.

This change came to me in a very commonplace situation. It was some time after my husband's death and I was marketing, a task I hated because I had no one to market for but myself — no one else's tastes to consider. At the vegetable counter I reached for some fresh asparagus. How my husband loved it. But the bunches were too big for one person and why bother to fix it just for myself? I trudged on. A part of the opera "La Traviata" poured in from the loud speaker. I heard it all the way to the meat counter. Then a lovely, long note was sung, a moment in the opera when my husband always caught my eye! Down the counter I saw some steaks. The first time after his death that I had gone to the freezer, I had found there two steaks. We had often bought them together on such an afternoon's marketing trip, bought them as a special treat. There were still two in my freezer at home.

Then I saw a teacher, one I wanted to avoid, so I slipped around a counter only to run into her at the next corner. I was deluged by her usual, lengthy and detailed accounts of problem students, long-ago research difficulties in biology, and her dreary and self-centered plans for the summer. I sidled along the aisles as she followed in spite of my saying I must get home. Finally escaping to the checkout stand, I waited my turn. As I stood there, I suddenly realized how little she had. Only books and bugs and herself to bleed over. For the first time I could honestly feel grateful for all that life had given me. For just a moment I accepted my loss *emotionally* rather than *mentally*.

Just then a close friend came into the store. I knew her husband was out of town so I asked her for dinner. "Let's see, I could have those two steaks and some biscuits with the red raspberry jam I made and hoarded for Dave and — of course, yes, some asparagus." And I was off to grab some and hurry home.

This illustrates so much more than the experience of being constantly reminded of a problem. This was an insight that changed my feelings. For a moment I changed from being sorry for myself, and forcing myself into the activity of marketing, to honestly feeling grateful for all that I had. Having released some emotion from my grief, I had made a small beginning in using genuine, motivating emotion for something besides grief. Then I continued to use that released emotion by extending the invitation to dinner — a spontaneous act that carried me out of myself — an example of the kind of thing you can do when it is possible to invest some emotional interest in something outside your problem. I had come to a time when for a short period I was not merely going through the motions of living. And with this came a change in my attitude toward the steaks, the jam and the asparagus. They were important for their own sakes; they were no longer preserved as memorials to my husband.

One such experience of acceptance cannot in itself mark a complete turning point, but it is a beginning. It shows that an inner change has taken place that could be called growth — a change which will be followed by other such experiences as you are able to find a new life.

To see the difference between the two motivations, going through the motions of doing something because you must and doing something because you want to—you have only to picture a boy making himself practice the piano, and then picture that boy practicing basketball. The same change can take place in relation to your problem. For a while you will probably do what you easily recognize as forcing yourself into activities mentally. Then, you will realize that you have become for short periods of time actually emotionally involved in something outside yourself.

Very gradually you will find that less of your emotional energy is tied up in your problem and more of it can be transferred to developing other interests. But you must go through the agony of dwelling mentally on your own problem in order to achieve the emotional relief which comes when you begin to make the gradual transition from mental to emotional motivation for your life.

THIRD . . .

As you go through these stages of adjustment do not fail to use the safety valve of crying. You will find that you are having an almost overpowering emotional experience, and you will be amazed to know how much better you will feel, how much better you will be able to cope, after a complete catharsis through tears.

Men have been trained to think of tears as feminine, but they pay dearly for this false restraint. A study made of men and women who were undergoing long-term stressful situations has shown that more men than women developed ulcers. It was thought this was because the men kept their emotions unexpressed within themselves, and women released theirs.

Think of crying as the emptying of a reservoir of damaging emotion. You will find after a good cry you will feel drained, but you will also probably have a surprising sense of relaxation and an even greater ability to cope.

Do not think of crying as a continuous state but as an emergency release. Try to choose the time and place to let yourself go. If possible cry when you are alone as you feel the pressure of emotion building up in you. If you do not empty yourself of your sorrow in private, you will find that you are using great discipline to keep yourself from spilling over and crying in public. I will never forget fleeing from a store to the privacy of the car when one of those moments struck me. When you are holding your emotion in, you must keep yourself so disciplined that you cannot turn your attention to anything else and so cannot make any progress in getting involved in other interests.

A friend had just heard of the approaching death of her little grandson from the slow, deteriorating disease of leukemia. She was also facing a week of final examinations. She had talked to me, and I told her about the release of crying. She said she would have felt it was wrong to cry, but when she went home, she gave in to her feelings and cried long and hard. Although she felt empty and tired afterwards, she found she was able to study for her finals.

FOURTH . . .

Another aspect is the importance of being in top physical health. You know yourself that when you are well, anything seems possible, and when you are not, the simplest activity requires great effort. Right now there is nothing you *want* to do, and you need all the help you can get from your body. Go to your doctor and have a physical examination. Sometimes an experience such as you are going through in itself brings on physical problems. If your doctor finds you have any difficulty, do whatever he suggests to correct it. An old physical difficulty of mine flared up after my husband's death, and I had to have an operation. If your doctor finds you in good physical condition, be very grateful.

Daily exercise is important too — walking, swimming, anything that you enjoy doing that encourages good circulation and that tires you so that you can sleep.

One other step that you may not have thought of is getting an emotional check from a psychiatrist. Some months after my husband died, I felt I had made so little progress in adjusting to his loss that I went to a psychiatrist. In my one and only conference with him, I learned two things. First he showed me how to handle my emotions better. And second, when I asked when I should see him again, he said I wouldn't have to come back because I'd now be able to handle my problem by myself. How encouraging and welcome that was to hear when I had been sure that I would never again be like myself.

FIFTH . . .

Seek a purpose outside yourself, one important enough to absorb the involvement you once invested in your former life. Such a purpose cannot be decided on mentally. It usually evolves naturally from a variety of trial activities. This point is inspiringly discussed in *Man's Search for Meaning,* a paperback by Viktor Frankl. In it Dr. Frankl, an outstanding European psychiatrist, describes his prison-camp experience with great insight and shows the important part that purposefulness played in his personal survival.

For over three years of prison life, Dr. Frankl had none of the usual supports that we take for granted. He did not know whether his wife was alive or not. He had barely enough food to give him strength to carry out the endless manual labor assigned to him. He worked, slept, and ate in the cold of the German winters. With several men in one wooden bunk, they were disturbed in their sleep as they changed position and snored in one ceaselessly uncomfortable mass. Illness was disregarded by the prison officials, many of whom were sadistic tyrants. His companions deteriorated into mere animals. But the worst of all aspects of the prison experience was the uncertain outcome of his life. We can stand certain physical pain, like that of a dentist's drill, if we know how long it will last. However, for Dr. Frankl, the duration of the prison experience and the very outcome of the war were unknown.

He said he survived because of his desire to live to rewrite a manuscript on psychiatry that had been taken from him and destroyed when he entered prison. It was this purpose that pulled him through the dehumanizing prison-camp experience.

To illustrate the importance of purpose in life, Dr. Frankl told of a friend in camp who confided to him that he had dreamed he would be released from camp on a certain date. As that date drew near, there was no sign of Germany's defeat and the friend's release. With the loss of hope and purpose, he grew ill, went into a coma on the date he had dreamed of, and died the following day. He was released from camp on the date he dreamed of but not in the way he had anticipated.

Dr. Frankl's book is recommended reading for anyone suffering a crisis, for his account can inspire motivation to find a way out of a problem by eventually learning to care about something outside oneself.

One man who became involved with an other-than-self activity was a grocer whose business failed. He felt defeated by his inability to "make a go of things", as he put it, and it became evident that he was not in demand in other firms to which he applied. But he got very interested in a Boy Scout troop. The boys did some outstanding work in leathercraft, and after a canoe accident, two of them were decorated for saving a boy from drowning. Also the man himself recognized that some of the boys were changing. They seemed to be more sure of themselves and better able to make decisions. The grocer, in an emergency, was asked temporarily to take the position of Director of the Community Center where the scout troop met. This developed into a permanent appointment. And the grocer who had been a defeated businessman found himself a fulfilled and important community leader. He couldn't have anticipated that such a thing would happen to him, but he made a beginning, and, forgetting about himself, took advantage of every opportunity that came to him.

SIXTH . . .

Do not be surprised at the unexpected strength you will eventually experience if you face your problem squarely. Your sense of self will strengthen so that your self-image can adjust to the tragic circumstance that has come into your life.

When tragedy strikes, there are several paths for people to follow, and the path taken is unconsciously determined by the strength of the sense of self of each individual. The most defeating path is that of not caring. The divorcee who has no scars because there was no in-depth relationship to begin with. The handicapped person who gives up and won't work toward a new involvement with life. The jobless man who settles for public support.

These people with little useful sense of self and few satisfying experiences or relationships give up. They have been dwarfed in unseen ways, and do not feel responsible for themselves.

As St.-Exupéry said in *Wind, Sand, and Stars,* "To be a man is, precisely, to be responsible." He quotes an old gardener, who, on his deathbed, said, "Who is going to prune my trees when I am gone?" But defeated people have no such feeling of caring, no such feeling of their own importance.

A second path is one in which people may find in a tragedy, whatever that tragedy is, the most real and meaningful experience that has ever happened in a bland and unchallenging life. An untouched depth is discovered. Perhaps, in the tragedy, the life-giving power of individual attention has shown on one person through a therapist or a social worker. Perhaps another sees that a routine approach to problems will no longer work and he finds that he must use the whole of himself for the first time in his life. Whatever happens, he finds he is reborn when he is pushed out of his tepid and mediocre way of living.

And the third path is taken by those who were already on their way. Through tragedy they strengthened their sense of self.

If asked how tragedy affected them, those in the last two groups will say,

"I am more secure."

"I don't know how to express it, but I feel more whole."

"I feel stronger."

"I'm much more of a person."

"Somehow I have grown."

"I am more put together, whatever that means."

Anyone who has gone through a crisis knows exactly what each of these people is trying to say — that his sense of self has been strengthened and he has a new but a real involvement in life.

Author Peter Gordon shows how this kind of metamorphosis spread through a whole prison camp during the Korean War. In his book, *Through the Valley of the Kwai,* he tells how ordinary men from many countries, thrown together in a forced community, learned love for each other instead of hate. They brought from their jungle life an orchestra, an art gallery, a library, a university, and a church. They, as a group, "felt the touch of grandeur that can spring from adversity in the life of a single human being who has been tempered in the heat of tragedy."

But you must wonder, at this moment, how anything can help. The answer is in the world. Look around you and see living proof every day that people *do* surmount tragedies — that what happened to others can happen to you if you follow these principles and work in the right direction.

Strange as it seems, sorrow offers us one of our greatest opportunities for growth. But that growth should come gradually and spontaneously. If we are hurried or if we are dominated by patterns imposed from outside, our emotional healing does not follow its proper growth in its own good time.

The Crisis of Divorce

To live is good. To live vividly is better.
To live vividly together is best.
— Max Eastman

Before there can be an understanding of divorce, there must be some idea of what marriage *should* be. Nearly every marriage begins with hopeful expectation. But marraige is a different relationship from any other. Friendships develop and may wane. But no declaration of permanence has been made in a friendship, nor has a friendship been subjected to such close intimacy and constant adjustment as marriage. The two people in a marriage must agree on such basic decisions as how to spend time and money and how to raise children. Nor has a friendship been formed with the powerful pull of sex that camouflages as love. And a friendship is basically a simple person-to-person relationship while marriage includes relationships to whole families. Nor must friendship stand up to the "living happily ever after" romantic dream that marriage is supposed to fulfill. But a marriage must be a friendship too and not just a working relationship. It must be a friendship that interests both partners if it is to carry the two throughout a lifetime. Ideally your husband or wife is also your best friend.

Love has been defined as shared growth. It is seen as a "mesh of complementary needs, flowing into and out of one another," a caring as much for the partner's development as one's own. If love is shared growth, it is evident that marriage at its best requires two growing and maturing people. It has been said that marriage is not so much gazing into each others' eyes as looking outward together.

Marriage demands a relationship that supports but does not restrict, just as water supports the swimmer. This support is shown more in the quality of the marriage relationship than the quantity of contacts. The afterglow of a smile, a few words, or a midnight talk can sustain a good marriage if a husband is busy but wise enough to want to give marriage this kind of nurturing. This, of course, is true for a wife as well.

I visited in a home where the young husband had a full-time job and was also working on a Master's degree. This required a tight schedule that kept him involved most of his waking hours. But the obvious pleasure he took in slipping into the kitchen to hold his wife in his arms a moment, the fun he had from a romp with the children, his satisfaction at having his family together at dinner-time — these sustained his wife through her days, weeks, and months alone with her household work and their children.

When an inadequate person is a partner in a marriage, it obviously cannot mature as it should. One of the partners must do most of the adjusting. A woman, for years, managed a marriage to a homosexual alcoholic. She was so loving and hopeful that she never would have given up the marriage, but the husband himself finally left her and joined the world of homosexuals.

Often a marriage involves two perfectly fine people who simply do not grow and develop at the same rate or in the same direction. A woman, young, beautiful and growing, was married for five years to a good man who had a range of interests that expanded only from A to B. Hers spanned almost the whole gamut of life itself. When she left him, he was amazed and hurt. She had outwardly adjusted to his slow tempo and limited involvements so that he was perfectly content and could not understand that his focus of interest had in it only a fraction of the potential that was bursting to be expressed in her life. This imbalance is often found when a man, stimulated by his work, leaves behind him a wife involved with an unrelieved *Küche and Kinder* existence. There is no growing together here; rather a gradual growing apart.

The "Dear Abby" column is full of letters from women grown desperate because their husbands are glued to TV sports programs or go out to play golf or hunt on their only free day. The husbands are frankly enjoying a day of relaxation after a week's stimulation or worry at work.

The wives, after a week tied at home and largely alone, may be bored and want variety and companionship. Sometimes the wives nag and become people who do not attract attention from their men. And so a vicious circle is established — one that is quite common in American marriages. A French grandmother who understood this danger said to her lovely young granddaughter on the eve of her wedding, "Remember, petite, to find some way to stay happy. For when you are sad, you grow plain, when you are plain, you grow bitter; when you are bitter, then you are disagreeable, and a disagreeable woman has nothing — neither friends, love, nor contentment."

Many women are completely fulfilled with keeping house and taking care of the children. Many are not. Some women adjust by supplementing their domestic lives. they may take classes, get a full- or part-time job or do any of the many activities which nourish them. But any woman who is not happy with herself can't be a good wife and a good mother and make her husband and children happy. If a woman is bored, frustrated, and irritated, she cannot be a source of comfort, joy, and love. And that's what a man wants to come home to after the unpredictable ups and downs or the gray monotony of a day at work. A man who is an office manager was asked if he minded his wife having a part-time job. "Mind? No! This keeps her the kind of person I fell in love with! And that's what I want more than anything else in the world." And that is what marriage should be — something more than either person would have been alone. And if a man thrives on the stimulus and variety of work and home, why shouldn't a woman — if that variety is what she happens to need? Anyone who fulfills his or her needs is much more likely to help those around him fulfill theirs.

A widow of a well-known physician told me of their solution to this problem. Her husband took one week from every month to be with his wife. They stayed home and enjoyed their family and friends or they went away for a week's holiday. She told me that once when they were having dinner at a famous hotel an old gentleman stopped at their table to say, "Either you two are very remarkable people or you are not married. It is rare to see a couple of middle-age having as much fun together as you are." And without further comment he walked on. But few couples can finance such an arrangement. And unless a man is in his own business or in a partnership as this physician was, he is not free to be away from it one week a month. However, this couple's solution illustrates the emotional need to cultivate a growing relationship in marriage rather than one based on mundane daily decisions involving money and which TV program to watch.

There are many couples who manage a marriage because the relationship has become patterned so that each can fit into it comfortably if not devotedly. In such marriages the concern for the partner may be checked off by a standard ritual that was first prompted by some moment of spontaneous caring. It may have been carrying the laundry for a tired wife or laying out slippers and the evening paper for a returning husband, but the first, fine, careless giving that began the ritual has withered. The ritual remains to make one partner feel noble by performing the standard service for the other. Yet from a growing relationship between two people there springs a flow of kindness that shows constant awareness of the other. This fresh and surprising evidence of rapport really says, "Here I am," one who quite naturally sees things from your point of view and sees where you need to be supplemented.

Some marriage partners are lucky enough to grow and change so that each is what the other would have chosen at new periods of development. I know an unusually happy couple, the marriage a second one for each of them. They would never have been attractive to each other in their teens. He was a dancing fool and she was sensibly devoted to good works. But by middle age they had grown toward a middle ground, met and married.

An example of this in reverse is the marriage which went along well for twenty years but came to an end when the husband retired from the service. He was lost when the service activities and the respect due his rank were removed from his life. His security was not within himself but in the outward prop of the service structure. He became quiet and almost shy and eventually took a routine, mediocre job. His wife was the same person he had enjoyed all those years, but her whole lifestyle was no longer becoming to him. Through no fault of her own, she now outshone him. After several years it was evident that he had settled for remaining the retiring person he had become and she would not change artificially to supplement him — and so, they were divorced. The divorce merely recognized the almost separate lives they had begun to live.

A more common example of a partner not filling a need is that of a man who was going through the crisis of middle age. He felt he needed a young woman to give him a sense of youth that was no longer appropriate for him. His fifty-five-year-old wife could not satisfy his need for a fling, the kind of gay fun he had never had in his youth. So they were divorced. He has had affairs with two younger women but has not married either.

However, couples who do not grow together may work hard on the separate parts of their mutual business — she on the home and children, he on earning the money to support them all. Consequently the business end of marriage is fine: the budget, recipes, lawn care, music lessons. But friendship and love and growing and becoming persons together seem to be lost in tehniques and routine. Then the children leave home, the couple's most important mutual project is over. Because the children are gone, the wife may face a crisis that the husband is not very much concerned with because he is no longer basically interested in her as a person. He may face his crisis later, retirement, to which she will be equally indifferent. Without realizing it, they have merely carried on a workable partnership that is no longer needed. When the failure of the relationship is revealed, the budget, recipes, lawn care and music lessons do not matter because there is no enduring relationship that these specifics supplemented— a marriage of bricks with no mortar. No wonder such marriages fall apart.

Even social life does not bring a couple together. They may go to a party together but of course they spend most of their time there communicating with other people. Some couples unconsciously avoid being alone, for they have little relationship aside from their mutual concern for the children and the household. And sex in itself is not the answer. It is much easier to make love than a relationship. In the long run a good relationship is the mainstay of a real marriage no matter what problems come.

One couple stumbled onto this very important truth about marriage. They were having trouble communicating, and their whole marriage relationship was edgy. Then they were left alone for two weeks when the grandparents took the children on a trip. And to their surprise and pleasure, they resumed their early marriage relationship as persons and became a couple again. Their children, attractive and loved, absorbed the parent's time and attention, leaving them little to invest in each other. This experience came early enough in their marriage for them to realize that they were starving the relationship between them. Now they plan their own time together every night after the children are in bed, every week in a special evening together, and every year in a vacation alone. The grandparents are delighted to keep the children during these vacations, and everybody in the family has an enriching change — parents, children, grandparents. Of course they still do many things with the children, but their relationship to the children is better because they have taken the trouble to cultivate their relationship to each other. Couples who do not take the trouble to do this may find that they are not building a marriage so much as they are building a divorce.

But there are many couples who take the trouble to keep their marriage alive. One couple goes camping and leaves the work-a-day world behind. Another dresses up, goes to a fancy hotel, orders a beautiful dinner, and has breakfast sent to their room. I recently saw these two happy ones at a handsome restaurant having an evening out together with drinks, wine, dinner. And they talked, really communicating, unaware that anyone else was around. He courted; she was wooed. They were grandparents, but also friends and lovers.

Such people obviously enjoy being together. And because of their joy in each other, they are giving their children the best possible example to follow in their own marriages.

A good marriage goes well beyond the work routine. I visited a friend for a few days, and during my stay she laughed at herself for being such a bungler in the kitchen. When I got home, I had the satisfaction of writing her that while she might be a bungler in the kitchen, her relationships showed that she was a howling success in living.

When you married, both you and your spouse felt sincerely that you wanted the same fulfillments from the relationship. But as life continued, you found that some of these were only temporary. So if you, as a couple, are not doing well in the art of living together, go to a marriage counselor or understanding minister, priest or rabbi, or perhaps to a couple that has a good marriage. The title of the person or persons you consult isn't so important as their wisdom and evidence of success in making a go of life. As a couple, you should take all possible steps to preserve your marriage rather than let it go by default. There is an excellent book, *The Mirages of Marriage* by Lederer and Jackson, which shows how to analyze and come to understand your own marriage. If you feel there is something wrong, if you want to put it right, if you care enough about your marriage to dare open yourselves to changing and growing, you should get the book and follow its procedures.

The problem is that people do not change unless they are so unhappy and uncomfortable with themselves that they *have* to change. It might be that an individual would prefer to continue to get by as the person he or she is and lose the marriage, than to go through the pain of growth. However, as one psychologist put it, "We regularly underestimate the resiliency of the human psyche and so underestimate the capacity of the normal personality to adjust." People *can* change. One partner may want to get professional help, but the other balks. The defense of a person with little inner security is to say that there is nothing wrong with him or her so why go see a marriage counselor or anyone else?

The image that some women have of themselves is so limited and so rigid that they cannot imagine themselves as anything but housewives. So they hang onto a marriage that has gone flat. An army wife allowed herself to gain seventy pounds and paid no attention to the perfectly evident affairs that her husband carried on — but she hung on to the only role she knew, for she had no identity of her own outside of marriage. He had tired of feeding her meager ego and stayed with her only because she threatened to "sock him" financially if they were divorced. They had no marriage at all! But their fear of the unknown was greater than their boredom with the dead center of their complete frustration.

Although this is an extreme case, many a person with less obvious problems has stayed in a marriage because of the difficulty of changing a self image. So inertia takes over and they continue, giving their lives to a relationship that has ended.

An accountant did well, exceptionally well, in business, but he was a failure in personal relationships. He did not have a single personal friend. When he sent out announcements of his daughter's marriage, not one person on his list even acknowledged the announcement. In his own mind, his sense of superiority and confidence in business carried over into the personal area of his life, and no one could have persuaded him that he needed help as a human being because the business machine part of him functioned so well. He failed most of all by not living.

The disussion so far has centered around causes and preventions of divorce. To put it in simple terms, the cause is almost always some aspect of emotional immaturity, an important part of which may be the poor choice that began the marriage. Understanding the cause may in some cases lead to prevention of a divorce. But if you have reached a dead end in trying to save your marriage, save yourself and turn to divorce.

If a marriage does have to end in divorce, one person is usually more hurt by it than the other, a feeling that is caught in the following poem:

NEGATIVE NUMBER

Our coming together
    has made it quite clear;
One plus one equaled
    (most beautifully) two;
Then how does it happen
    my darling, my dear,
That one minus one
    is so
    much less than nothing
(and I so diminished
by being subtrated from you?)

— *Carol Burdick Hudson*

Yet with the hurt and loneliness you may be experiencing, even negative feeling is better than no feeling at all. William Faulkner speaks of this when he says that between grief and nothing, he would choose grief.

Your adjustment to a divorce will be good in direct proportion to the strength of your sense of self and your resulting capacity to change your self-image. These are your most valuable assets.

Divorce is in many ways like the death of a partner and there are some useful ways of looking at the two together.

It is true that divorce may be easier than death if there has been a gradual, rather than a sudden, change in the relationship. If this has happened, much of the shock of adjusting has been experienced, and perhaps by the time the divorce actually takes place, there is a sense of relief at being through with the marriage — at least through with trying to make something of it. Having limped along with a relationship — having coped with indifference, alcoholism, other women or other men, having compromised, made excuses, or been embarrassed — you may find that divorce is actually welcome. It is amazing the sense of relief there can be in being even with the world, shed of unpredictability, done with a situation that had to be cleared up before a life alone could be built without the millstone of a poor relationship. Coping with an opposing force takes a lot of energy.

But there are many other ways in which divorce is more difficult than the death of a partner.

I have rarely talked with a divorced person who did not himself feel he was somehow inadequate. A need to keep on trying has maintained some people for years before they resorted to divorce, for they felt that surely there was something that could be done to make the relationship work. The problems of one couple began when he was jolted out of a pattern of life he had been able to handle. He was released from a position that he was dependent on for his sense of worth. The loss of his position removed the most important support that propped up his inwardly weak sense of self. Almost overnight he withdrew into himself. For five years their marriage faltered, and they finally agreed to divorce. In spite of the almost impenetrable wall behind which the husband hid himself, his wife had a great sense of final inadequacy in her inability to develop a good relationship with him.

A sense of failure bothered the wife for years until she

began to see that he had become a complete recluse, bitter and shut off from all human contact that demanded any adjustment from him. He was a person she never could have made a life with unless he had psychiatric help, but he refused any form of counseling. The loss of a job and the blow to his self-image had destroyed the façade that hid his weak sense of self and inability to adjust.

Another factor, an emotional and practical one, that makes divorce more difficult than death is the disagreeable haggling that may go on over the division of property or children— the tangible evidence of the meshing of the relationship of two people.

Deciding on what to do about the children is the most difficult of these divisions because they are not commodities that can be divided, like furniture. Their feelings and future good are involved. Through no fault of their own, they are being subjected to a serious change in their lives. This is another major cause for a sense of failure on the part of those going through divorce. Each might say, "What lack in me has brought this tragedy on my children?"

Children of divorced parents do have difficulties because they have to cope with their own confused feelings as well as the sometimes conflicting and negative feelings of their parents. A book helpful for them is *The Boys and Girls Book on Divorce* by Richard A. Gardner, a child psychiatrist. It is a simply-written book so that children can understand it, and there are examples of typical scenes that illustrate for younger children some of the situations they may encounter.

Much of what has been said about adjustment for adults is reflected in this book for children. Dr. Gardner advised children to accept the *reality* of the divorce and not daydream of the time the father may return home or make up difficulties that may not happen. He particularly assures them that the divorce is not due to anything they have done. He tells them that it has taken place because their parents no longer want to live together. He urges children to talk to their parents about the divorce and ask them all the questions that they have about it as problems come up. And he tells them to cry if they feel like it because that will make them feel better.

If helping your children understand the divorce is part of your divorce adjustment, this book should help you. It discusses all sorts of feelings that children have about which you may not even be aware, and it gives you an understanding of how to help your children cope with those feelings.

In addition to problems in connection with children, there are also problems with other people to be considered in a divorce; relatives and close friends who often take sides and so become alien to one partner in the marriage. Through divorce you may lose human resources that you are used to depending on.

Even decisions about material things are difficult. The dividing of a house, furnishings, money, and arranging alimony and child support are usually disagreeable because the divisions that are made set up a permanent structure of money and material objects that may in one case spell future security to a wife and a future burden to a husband, or in another case, starvation support for a wife. I know a husband who, typical of many, is living two thousand miles from his wife, and who simply ignores any legal communications relating to a divorce because a final settlement would mean taking financial responsibility — something he does not want to do.

There is one other aspect of divorce which makes it more difficult than the death of a spouse, and it is a subtle but vital psychological one. People do not make basic emotional adjustments unless they are so uncomfortable that they have to. After the death of a husband or wife, unless the survivor chooses permanent defeat, there is no path open but to grow emotionally. This is a painful process, but eventually a healing one. It is forced on the bereaved because of the finality of death.

In divorce there is no such finality. There are bits of hope that can prevent you from facing up to this painful emotional growth. Maybe he or she will find single life unbearable. Maybe the other man or other woman will prove to be inadequate. Maybe he or she will be sick or hurt and need you. Maybe — maybe — the maybes you can find are endless. I know a woman who went through three years of hoping that her husband would again turn to her. And in that time she failed to take a single useful step toward making an adjustment. She refused to face the burden of rejection and the grief of separation and camouflaged her problem with sleeping pills and drink. The emotional torture she experienced was so severe that she had what is vaguely and commonly referred to as a "nervous breakdown", complete with psychiatrists and institutional care.

If you were to go through the painful growth demanded of adjustment to divorce and if, as happens in rare instances, you were to remarry the same person, you would then be a stronger and better person as a marriage partner. The growth in you would have given your remarriage a greater chance of success than if both had remained the same persons whose weaknesses may have caused the divorce in the first place. However, to grow in the hope of remarrying the same person would be too great a gamble, and such a perspective would in itself limit your chance of going through a thorough and useful adjustment. Should no remarriage take place, you would unconsciously feel a sense of failure, while growth for growth's sake would provide a step to so many new strengths and experiences that your opportunities for fulfillment would be increased, whether within marriage or not.

In addition to growing emotionally after a divorce, you must change in practical ways.

If you are a woman and if you have children, you may have to get a job, provide care for the children, move to a smaller or at least a less expensive place to live. Your life will be devoted largely to work and children, unless you do not need to work. Your social contacts may change from contacts with neighbors to ones with co-workers. If you do not have children, you will probably return to whatever your life was before your marriage, usually school or work.

If you are a man, you are likely to have fewer practical adjustments to make than a woman. Your work life is established, and probably you will not be given the responsibility for children. You may have to live in a different home and perhaps form different friendships, but there certainly is no dearth of women if you are interested. There are so many more single women than men that you will probably find that you are sought after. But you must adjust to the new financial arrangement with which you have to live. Because you are now supporting two households, usually neither can be maintained on the same standard of living you have been used to. In addition, you probably must get used to doing laundry, housework and errands. Another of the difficult aspects for you is the unnatural and planned basis on which you will see your children. It is awkward for you to manufacture activities to enjoy with them because such activities cannot be a part of your everyday life together

No matter whether you are a man or a woman, you will have to face the reality of the divorce. You do this by making yourself thoroughly aware of it, *mentally*. You will be forced into this by the whole new life you will have to live, for nearly every activity of your life will be changed. Do not maintain any reservations about the finality of it. Face its reality. If this is difficult, do not be tempted to avoid the pain with liquor or drugs. These will only postpone the healing hurt you must experience if you are to make an eventful adjustment.

One thing your close friends can do for you is to give of themselves in encouraging you to talk to them about every ramification of the divorce that you want to share. Your talking about it, forming the words, hearing your own voice say the things you must come to believe, will help you.

There will be a time, after you have come to accept the idea of the divorce *mentally,* when you will gradually come to accept it *emotionally.* At this point it will begin to be easier because your emotions are being freed from the marriage, and you will find you are open to becoming involved in other activities. This change, *mental* to *emotional* acceptance, marks a major turning point in your adjustment.

It will be hard to do, but try not to talk to more than a few close friends about the details of the divorce. In the first place, only your real friends are interested in you and your divorce except as a source of gossip. But do not allow yourself to reveal even to close friends details that you do not want repeated. There is often a lot that is ugly in a divorce which is better not publicized. There may be a day when you will be sorry you revealed too much of your story to anyone. And do not be surprised if some friends listen sympathetically but do not take sides by indicating either sympathy or blame. They may simply nod compassionately.

After a divorce, it is wise to operate on the principle that you keep yourself going in order to be a person for your own sake — not especially to attract a mate. If being a person is important to you, this naturally means you keep up your mind, your contacts, your looks. You'll usually want to do more than shell peas and get the whitest wash on Main St. if you're a woman; more than make a nightly ritual of eating the blue plate special and watching TV if you're a man.

Your life should revolve around keeping yourself the

kind of person who likes himself. It then will follow that you will be the kind of person who likes others. If this description fits you, you will have a kind of "que sera sera" attitude about remarriage rather than centering on a purposeful prowl for a mate.

But you may come out of divorce a rather battered person — one not too sure of your own worth. In addition, whatever brought on the divorce may have progressively diminished you until you may feel your are incompetent in many areas of your life. But having been released from the circumstances that engulfed you in your marriage, you are probably in for a pleasant surprise as other aspects of your self begin to emerge.

But to discover these other aspects, you need a period of emotional rehabilitation as much as you need a physical one after an illness. This means you'll probably want to begin to date.

But can you face going back to dating, after diapers and paying the mortgage? It's a role you haven't been in for so long that you feel you're entering another world. It may be frightening to be on the loose again. However, you need to try yourself out with dates that provide the give-and-take of relationships with a variety of people. If you have no children you probably live alone, for there are few group living set-ups for solo people in our society except in large cities. You've learned what it can be like to have Saturday nights by yourself. And although you hated the arguments and fights of your marriage, at least they were strong involvements with another person. Now you may subsist on a too steady diet of "How are you?", and you long for relationships with some reality to them. Casual contacts aren't enough. You need to learn through experience with people to trust your emotions again, because you found them none too reliable in leading you to and through your marriage. And socially, whether you believe it or not, you may be an unconscious threat to some of the none-too-stable couples with whom you associate. So you turn to other solo people and dating for companionship.

Society has a way of providing organizations to meet individual needs. The singles apartment buildings in large cities, the singles weekend trips, Parents Without Partners, and singles clubs have all developed since divorce has become a widespread reality in our society. These organizations all provide initiation into the unfamiliar world of singles, and they can be very useful.

You probably hadn't thought of it, but you and many others may have married the first time before you'd finished jelling as a person. You perhaps married before you knew who you were — while you were still in the role of a son or daughter in your own family and before you had a definite sense of self. Now divorced, you have a chance to pick up again on your growth as an individual.

All this means that you owe yourself time to date after a divorce. You need to rebuild your self esteem and learn that you can still be attractive and responsive to other people. Then you need a second period in which you allow your sense of self to develop. It may have gotten lost in the marriage you have just ended.

I saw a young woman experience these two periods.

During the first, recovery from divorce, she grew used to herself as a single person. She lived with another girl and developed a new personal and social life. However, during this time she dated and even encouraged two entirely inappropriate men, one an emotionally unstable and immature man and the other a homosexual.

Then she went through another long period in which she lived alone and continued the trial and error of getting to know a great variety of people. Finally she came into a truly glorious marriage. But I doubt that she would have recognized her second husband as someone right for her immediately after her divorce. And perhaps in that early period, she would not have been mature enough to interest him.

As you become more aware of dating patterns, you'll notice that perhaps you and other couples who seem perfectly congenial may break up, change partners, go together for a while, then switch again. Probably one partner is such a pattern has gone through several years of dating around and has come to terms with him or herself and is emotionally ready to marry again. But the other one of the partnership has been free only a few months and feels trapped and thwarted at the very idea of a permanent relationship. There's a time when you're emotionally ready to form a good, permanent relationship, and you'll recognize it. But don't hurry it.

It even suits some people to look forward to remaining single because they like freedom and variety. But actually there's no use planning that you will or won't marry again. You have to live through whatever comes to you and know you'll have a good life either way if you can come through divorce as a whole person — not one destroyed or stunted. Life should be an adventure in self-discovery which may take place either within or without a marriage. A good book to read on the aftermath of divorce is *The World of the Formerly Married* by Morton Hunt.

A delightful and twice-divorced woman was asked if she wanted to marry again. She answered thoughtfully and seriously. "For my own sake I'll keep myself as interesting and attractive as I can. And if a marriage and the joy of companionship happen, I'll be very happy. But if you mean to ask if I'm going out for another marriage — No. There is something about the spirit of the hunt that does not foster the kind of relationship that would interest me."

One thing to remember — if you need to, cry. Through divorce you are tearing your life apart as truly as you would if you had lost your partner through death. Empty yourself of your negative emotions through tears, but do not make crying a way of life on a long-term basis. This applies as well to men as to women. The safety valve of tears is remarkable, but cry in private and avoid overflowing in public where you will involve other people.

Do not forget the suggestion that you check your physical and perhaps even your emotional health, for you need to be at your best to get through all the adjustments you must make in going through a divorce. If, over a long period, you cannot make an adjustment to divorce, you will then need to see a counselor. You may discover that you have a basic problem which you were not aware of until you were unable to adjust to a marriage relationship and a divorce.

Through your divorce you should have learned a great deal about marriage and what it takes to create a good one, and you should also have learned a great deal about yourself. Wait to consider remarriage until you as a person have settled. There are worse things than not being married, and one of them is being married to someone for the wrong reason.

Because of your divorce you have a chance at a new beginning in your life, a beginning you are coming to as a more seasoned person. You will want to make an emotional adjustment to your experience that will give you a good basis for your whole future, one that is not bitter or unrealistic. You have suffered, and whether you like it or not, suffering is useful if it is the basis for personal growth. Use this suffering to its greatest advantage.

A Physical Handicap

When I think of physical handicaps, I picture two people
— one a handsome, successful man who goes about town
on his important business with a limp. He lost a leg and
wears an artificial one. The other is a bored-looking older
man who frequently can be seen sitting slumped up
against one of the downtown store fronts. He displays a
trouser leg, empty below the knee, and he has lead pen-
cils to sell in the hat he holds out to the passing crowd.
Together these two illustrate a recognized truth about
physical handicaps: *the capacity to adjust to the handicap
is more important than the degree of the handicap.* Helen
Keller surely testified to this principle.

Loss and change in many forms are part of human experience from birth to death. Someone with a physical handicap is faced with a major adjustment, and will find that a sense of self is the greatest asset in working through this change.

An adjustment to any tragic circumstance is much more than difficult. There are times when it seems unsurmountable. Yet it is only recently that doctors and psychologists have realized how desperately people need information and help in facing physical changes.

Anyone who has ever tried to lose weight, had his hair dyed, worn a wig or toupee, gotten a lift from a new suit or dress, has been reacting to the natural need to look his best. When I was no longer young, I had to have my thyroid removed. On hearing I needed the operation, my first question was a silly one — "Will it leave a scar?" an effect that was entirely beside the point. The point was that I needed the operation. On looking back I am surprised at the unconscious vanity that prompted me even to think of a scar under the circumstances. But physical appearance is important to us. We get used to looking as we do, and we do not want to change our appearance unless it is for the better. Yet any person could suddenly suffer a physical disability. No one is immune.

A plastic surgeon said he has observed that even people who sought out and planned for a change in their appearance took days to accept it, although appearance was improved. If this is true, what a difficult adjustment it is to accept a sudden physical change that is not an improvement. Even a small and temporary facial blemish bothers someone whose physical image is especially important. A major and permanent change in the body requires a major and permanent psychological adjustment. The more emotion invested in the lost part or the lost function, the harder it is to make the change. A facial disfigurement would be more difficult to meet than the loss of a foot, which would be inconvenient and perhaps painful, but not so great a blow to the image of the very self. The book, *Tell Me That You Love Me, Junie Moon*, shows how magnificently Junie makes an unusual kind of life for herself in spite of her disfigurement. She shows she is an independent soul with a strong sense of self which is operating behind her kindly heart and twisted features.

Studies have been made of people who have suffered major physical handicaps, and it has been found that a large percentage have made a good adjustment. This is partially due to man's amazing resiliency. It has further found that those who did not do as well as they thought they should could get help from a counselor in making an adjustment to their disability. These people had an unsuspected weak spot in their ability to adjust that might not have been revealed at all if they had not had to face an unusual and tragic change in their lives.

Adjusting to living with severe chronic illnesses such as heart trouble, arthritis, diabetes, or emphysema can be quite as difficult for people as an adjustment to any other physical change. The change that must be accepted by such people is a loss of a sense of total well-being and the constant reminders of the illness in the form of diets, medication, treatments, and limited activity. Many people in this situation need to express their feelings, rebellious and angry as they may be, and they frequently need support and assurance from their doctors and families. Such people may or may not be able to continue a normal or nearly normal life, but the constant discipline for some becomes almost unbearable, and they may disregard the limitations which sustain health, if not life itself.

Usually, the first reaction to physical change is "Oh no! Not me!" And unless the change is clearly permanent, such as the loss of a limb, there is always the perfectly reasonable hope that time and treatment may return you to normalcy. You really do not know what the eventual outcome will be until you begin to realize that therapy, doctors, operations, hearing aids or glasses, can do no more for you. One great problem with this first period is that your very disability often keeps you inactive, and you have to lie in bed where you have too much time to think and too little outlet in physical activity for your tremendous frustrations.

The greatest torture came to a friend of mine who was completely immobile in a body cast for months as a result of an accident that had injured her and killed her husband. She had time to think and grieve, but too often no one to talk to and no activity to occupy her even for a moment. Added to her grief over her husband's death was the terrible uncertainty of her own future. Would she walk again? What deformity would she carry with her the rest of her life? Drugs helped soothe her, but the immobility, near isolation and her own physical weakness made her experience cruel to bear.

A special problem during the first period of facing a disability is often the bewildering feeling of helplessness that strikes. You have been independent and able to go where you wanted to or look at whatever interested you. You were able to satisfy your own needs — get a drink, go to the bathroom, light a cigarette, feed yourself, or scratch. But now you may need help with almost every movement. You are, of course, frightened. This is especially hard to face because, at a low ebb physically, you find that everything is hard to cope with when you have little vitality with which to meet it.

There is not only the immediate frustration of limitation and helplessness, but there is the projected future to consider. How will people feel about you and treat you? What degree of normalcy will you again reach? Whatever fears you have, ask your doctor to give you a reasonable idea of what you can expect. Ask him specific questions. You may be worrying about some difficulties which may be misconceptions on your part. But do not be surprised if your doctor himself does not know what ultimate degree of normalcy you will have. According to a young woman permanently crippled in an accident, "You must face the immediate future with flexible expectations." You will make small gains through almost imperceptible day-to-day changes that eventually may build up to a major improvement.

You may be tempted to refuse to believe that you won't again be your former physical self. The only way one girl could get through the first year of her blindness was to hope to herself that she would eventually see. But as time went on she realized that she was not going to be able to, and she finally began to work at learning Braille, something she should have allowed to absorb her much sooner. She would have had a hard year, at best, becoming used to her new self, but she would not have spent that year in aimless and frustrating waiting based on a false hope. Facing reality is the only way to meet any problem.

An important thing you must do is express your feelings about your physical change — anger, frustrations, or fear. You may have any one of several first reactions, none of which should be anything but temporary. The almost universal first reaction to severe physical change is one of depression and anxiety. You may even think, "This frankly seems just too much for me to accept right now. I don't know how I'll manage. I'll have to see."

You may refuse to admit your despair over what has happened to you, and so you go through the motions of a kind of surface acceptance. This is natural on a short-time basis but your real feelings must come through eventually. A boy paralyzed in an auto accident who maintained this stiff-upper-lip attitude for weeks, finally broke down with a flood of acceptance and tears. In any adjustment, we simply cannot afford to lie to ourselves about how we feel. Emotion that is driven underground may cause emotional damage or may prolong the adjustment.

I'll never forget visiting a young man who had been crippled by polio. As he lay in the hospital, he began to think out loud. "I don't like the prospect of living in a wheelchair any better than the next fellow. But I have figured out two things. One is that my interests are such

that I don't have to walk. I want to teach and I can certainly continue to go to school and learn to do that. Then,
although my folks aren't actually rich, they have enough
so they can pay for whatever I need to supplement me."
Having sorted out the possibilities in his future, he then
turned all his energy into his rehabilitation. Today he has
a wife and children and is a top professor in a well-known
university. His chief use for his wheelchair is to get him
into the front row at conventions, for now he can manage
without it. Although he had not done research on how
he should react to his disability, he knew instinctively that
he had to take a realistic approach to his problem by recognizing his feelings about himself and by making some
practical plans for the future.

You may feel anger at the limitations you must face.
And like anyone else, you may not show it directly but
will get angry at other things or other people instead. I
know I do this. If I am upset in general, I am usually
cross at someone I can't see — like a telephone operator.
I will know perfectly well whatever it is I am complaining
about is not worth all the fuss I am making. But complaining expresses my worry or my anger over whatever is
really bothering me. Then I feel guilty and sorry for the
telephone operator or whoever has been on the other end
of the line! I do this because I cannot do anything about
the real thing that is bothering me, and apparently I have
to let worry out of my system in this cowardly way. Such
a safety device may be temporarily useful if other people
can take it, and if you know in your own heart what you
are doing — substituting anger about one situation that

you can't resolve for anger in another. But this would be a poor way to use a life, angry and disagreeable all the time, about something you cannot change.

As soon as you can begin to do something active about your problem — perhaps taking therapy or learning Braille — something that helps you get back some measure of self-sufficiency, you will find that the energy put into your anger will tend to be absorbed in taking some constructive steps toward making yourself independent again.

There are various ways that people have of making the mistake of avoiding recognition of their feelings. Two are typical. People may drink or take drugs and so avoid consciousness of their problem altogether. Or second, they may fill their minds with something else so they do not have to think about their problem. I made the mistake of immediately getting too busy after my husband died. The services for him were Tuesday and I went back to my teaching Thursday. This was in direct contradiction to what I should have done, which was to allow myself much more time to absorb what had happened to me. But I made this mistake before I learned something about how to handle my emotions. If you do not dwell on your problem mentally, you may prolong the time it takes to adjust to it, or you may submerge your feelings and so have difficulties because of your refusal to face the reality of your situation.

Having experienced the first perhaps violent reaction to the change in yourself, you enter a period of rehabilitation — physical, psychological, and perhaps even vocational — a period which may go on for months or years. Because you are probably in a program where people skilled in physical therapy help you, you may have the benefit of being in contact with others who can help you in the psychological and vocational areas.

In the final acceptance of a loss, there are three factors to consider — the importance of the loss to you, your capacity to adjust to your disability and the influence of the society in which you find yourself.

IMPORTANCE OF THE LOSS TO THE INDIVIDUAL

Any loss, even a so-called minor one, is important. But any sensory loss like that of sight or hearing is catastrophic because it governs a major part of communication with others. And, of course, a loss of a limb or loss of its function is central to your independence. Such losses as these would be difficult for all people to sustain.

However, there are losses that have special meaning for certain individuals depending on how they think of the body and its functions. Because of the sexual importance of a breast over and above its physiological function, some women who have a breast removed regard it as a turning point in their lives. It becomes a landmark. "That happened just before the surgery on my breast." "My breast operation was just ten years ago today." Or if such an operation is mentioned, they may say, "You know I had the same operation." Although the physical change does not show and although it does not in any major way incapacitate them, they seem always conscious of this change in themselves.

On removal of the prostate, some men may have the same type of reaction. However, many other people absorb such experiences and go on to live their lives as though they had had an appendectomy or other non-sexually-associated operation.

Other losses may seriously affect people vocationally. Obviously, a pianist, mechanic, or surgeon whose hands have been injured would have more serious problems of adjustment than would a salesman or lawyer suffering the same loss.

CAPACITY OF THE INDIVIDUAL TO ADJUST

This capacity has been covered in the discussion of the inner sense of self. *Its strength is your most important asset in making any adjustments* because it governs your capacity to change your self image.

As a result of a sense of self people have certain characteristics in greater or less degree which contribute to their security.

1. Secure people want to be loved for themselves. They want to be appreciated for what they are. A young man had just met a delightful older woman who was blind. After talking with her he said, "You are not handicapped. You are merely inconvenienced." What greater appreciation could he have shown for her as a person?

In a popular and very funny movie and stage play, *Butterflies Are Free,* a young man, attractive, self-sufficient, and blind, finds that he is truly loved by a young girl for his own sake. This play helps others see the handicapped as the real human beings that they are.

2. Secure people have a strong need to be independent — to achieve something through a task neither too easy or too hard — but to achieve by getting their teeth into something they are able to handle. A midwestern businessman is doing this by running a chain of sixteen stores from his wheelchair.

A friend of mine who is blind had a very wise mother. After several operations her doctor had to give her the verdict that her sight could not be saved. She was, quite naturally, terribly upset and was curt and cross in the doctor's office. On returning home her mother suggested that she write him a note apologizing for the way she had acted. She went to the typewriter and asked her mother to put the paper in for her. Instead her mother showed her how to put the paper in herself — her first step in independence down the long road of living the life she was to have. In her book, *None So Blind,* Bernice Clifton tells the whole story.

People with a desire to be independent wholeheartedly seek out everything that will help them get the best use of their physical selves — therapy, appliances, medication, diet. They want to live fully within the range of their capacities. Although the adaptation to a physical handicap requires constant effort of body and concentration of mind, they go at it with a will.

Some few people may *needlessly* stay at a dependent stage. If the handicap is crippling, it may be at the wheelchair stage. Perhaps they stop trying to improve because it requires such great effort, or because a wheelchair creates more attention and evokes more sympathy from others than braces and canes or crutches. There are a few such people, and they are those who have little inner reserve. Without a physical handicap, they might have lost a job, accepted unemployment compensation checks, or watched TV constantly and let it go at that.

3. Secure people aspire to act so that others will consider them as good, not as hostile or difficult. Some handicapped people, however, make negative adaptations to their limitations. They may attract attention to their handicap and demand pampering because of it. "Get me the paper." "I can't drive to the office alone."

They may consider the handicap an excuse for not taking responsibility. A veteran who himself is in a wheelchair said he felt that some men he had seen in the Veterans Hospital when he returned from Vietnam had given up and had not tried as hard as they might to become independent and make lives of their own. This man's opinion illustrates the point that some handicapped may tend to remain dependent.

Handicapped people who initially had a tendency to be hypochrondriacs will emphasize their limitations.

The people with positive characteristics will make the best adjustment possible to their handicap. They may even find strength they have never tapped before. Those with negative characteristics will have their difficulties. But being handicapped does not guarantee being strong and well-adjusted. The handicapped represent a cross section of all kinds of people. Some will do the best they can to make life good and others will just give up.

INFLUENCE OF SOCIETY

The handicapped must make their way in a society that has people in it with a great variety of attitudes toward them. In *Butterflies Are Free,* the blind boy says, "It isn't so much my blindness that's hard, but it's other people's reaction to it that makes it hard."

Some people are helpful to those with a handicap, thinking of them as individuals.

1. Such people frankly accept a handicap and do not dwell on it as though it were the only important and interesting thing about the other person. They let a handicapped person fend for himself as he is used to doing and do not go beyond offering casual help unless more is actually needed. They accept the person with a handicap as an independent, self-sufficient soul. A brilliant boy born with short arms and legs was genuinely accepted as "one of the boys." One day a crowd of his best high school friends, knowing he could swim, unstrapped his appliances and threw him into a lake, real evidence of his not being babied. He was elected vice-president of the student body, not because of his handicap, or in spite of it, but

because of what he was himself. Being vice-president had nothing to do with his handicap, if it can be called that, because long ago he had stopped thinking about it, and so had everyone else.

2. Such people enjoy friendships with others who are not handicapped. There is no reason to believe that the handicapped would necessarily be more congenial among themselves than any other arbitrary group, say all those six feet tall or all those born in February. They may have a physical limitation in common with other people who are handicapped as they are — but that is all.

When I was in school I had a friend, Mabel, who was a magnificent person. She had had polio and used a wheel-chair. The president of the Senior Class was a good friend of hers. There was a crowd of us who did a lot together. One of Mabel's great moment's was the night she went to the Senior Ball with the president of the class. Of course she did not dance, but the class president exchanged dances. (It was in the days of exchanging dances.) And she was attended by each girl's date.

3. Such people encourage any step toward independence on the part of the handicapped. They do this in the way that they would encourage achievement in anyone. "Your diving has certainly improved." Or "You've never before played that piece so well."

Pauline, whose mother was blind, knew a great deal about blind people and their needs. After her mother died, a friend of theirs suddenly went blind. As a part of her friendship and as a tribute to her mother, Pauline spent a month with her newly-blinded friend to help her learn such things as finding the way around her apartment, the tricks of identification that Pauline knew so well, marketing procedures, and using Talking Books, and so the newly-blinded friend learned to take steps toward her own independence.

A story goes that when Thomas Moore's beautiful wife was disfigured, she did not want him to see her. He was inspired to write this familiar and beautiful poem:

> Believe me if all those endearing young charms
> That I gaze on so fondly today
> Were to change by tomorrow and flee from my arms
> Like fairy gifts fading away,
> Thou wouldst still be adored
> As this moment thou art
> Let thy loveliness fade as it will.
> And around the dear ruin
> Each wish of my heart
> Would entwine itself verdantly still.

Although sentimental, these lines express the spirit of the emotional support that people who have been handicapped need to feel from those who love them. They naturally want to feel needed just as anyone else does. But they need special assurance.

On the other hand, some people are not helpful in their relationship to the handicapped.

1. Some people tend to do too much for the handicapped. They discourage their first tentative steps toward independence by anticipating their needs and supplying them. They may bustle about doing little things that emphasize the handicap more than they help the individual. They do not know any other way to show their concern, and it unconsciously makes them feel good.

2. Some people are artificially pleasant to those handicapped. A student in a wheelchair complained to me that he never saw the bad side of people. He said they were always kind and sweet as far as he was concerned, and he felt this was certainly a lopsided view of the world.

3. Many people seem to glorify youth and emphasize physical appearance. They make it seem that no one wears a size 22 dress or has a poor complexion or uneven teeth. They assume that each person is a perfect physical specimen. What a difficult world for the handicapped to fit into!

4. Too few people appreciate how much someone handicapped must extend himself in ways beyond the physical to become the person he is. Dr. Anne Carlson, the Director of the Crippled Children's Home in Jamestown, North Dakota, reports that at her school she emphasizes children's potential and develops their assets rather than thinking largely of their limitations. She herself was born without hands and feet, and she attributes her own ability to adjust to her family, "who did not devalue me although

I was different." They developed in her a sense of confidence and security by building her life around her many assets, and not her liabilities. Families, in their effort to help, may do too much for a handicapped member.

It has even been shown that in some cases a patient's physical improvement in the hospital has been partially lost when the patient returned home where too much was done for him. Again, in *Butterflies Are Free,* the young girl says to the boy's mother, "The more you help him, the more you hurt him."

5. Some people avoid or reject those who have a handicap as though that automatically disqualified them from being human beings.

6. Worse yet are those who stare!

7. Some make contact with the handicapped, but they keep their distance as though to say, "I'm not going to get involved."

8. And, for some reason, there are those who think that handicapped people are always serious. Some may be, but of course others have as much capacity for joy and fun as they ever had, and they want to express this part of themselves.

In a society that has in it some people who are not helpful in their relationship to you, as a handicapped person, you must go all the way in showing them you are a human being, not a peculiar person different from anyone else.

In other words, you not only have to make adjustments for yourself, but for others as well. It is hard enough for the handicapped to make their own place in society, but it is a sad truth that they must in addition make up for a lack of insight and empathy in others.

Not only do some people in society make it difficult for you to adjust to your handicap, but sometimes the family members who take care of you at home unknowingly also make it hard for you. Family members should be aware of the three warnings given in the first part of the chapter starting on page 115, WHEN SOMEONE YOU LOVE GOES THROUGH A CRISIS.

*   *   *

The world is full of remarkable people who have a life in spite of a physical handicap. A girl injured in an accident went through a rehabilitation period that was spread over several years. She reached a final stage where she could manage with braces and one crutch. She has earned a Master's degree, married, and had a baby. Others with similar injuries may still be moping in wheelchairs. She says, "Half the battle is in knowing finally what your limitations are. Then you can do something about them."

A star basketball player was born with one arm. He has always been accepted, and his coach says of him that, "He's just a hell of a kid. He never backed off from anything. He just decided he wanted to play basketball and that's what he did."

Much is being done for the handicapped now that make it possible for the great majority of them to lead good lives. Dr. Howard Rusk's book, *A World To Care For*, tells of the amazing rehabilitation that is being done today. In addition to physical rehabilitation, great personal development often takes place. The depth of this development is reflected in many instances in Dr. Rusk's book. One especially stands out. The wife of a man whose hands were blown off said, "Before Ernie lost his hands, he was an ordinary kind of fellow. Since he lost his hands, he's a great man." Many people experience just such a growth when they must learn to adjust to a handicap or to any other major problem that may face them.

A personnel officer, crippled by an accident in her teens, has lived most of her life in a wheelchair and has been successful as a professional woman and as a person. She believes that people must be judged as individuals. "We, the handicapped, don't want special breaks — only the opportunity to prove ourselves. Without hard knocks, you cannot begin to develop character." The same philosophy is expressed by a woman who was the victim of multiple sclerosis when she was in her teens. She became a wife and mother, a professional musician, an artist, and finally, blind and paralyzed, she is now a writer. She says, "You have to climb on top of the mountain or it will fall on top of you."

One of the most amazing stories I have known of is that of a thirty-eight-year-old friend disabled to the extent that he depended heavily on canes. After years of having been at a certain physical and personal plateau, he changed and moved ahead to an entirely new level of living as a result of experiencing an independence he had not before realized was possible. This happened to Hal during a week's vacation in a cabin part way up a rocky mountain. My husband and I invited Hal to join us there, but we warned him of the difficulties he would have even getting to the cabin from the car.

Hal came. His progress over the rocks leading to the cabin was slow, but he made it. The next morning he announced that he was going to take a walk. He returned exhausted but exhilarated. He had gone up the mountain a mile and back and said going up was not so bad because he could lift his game leg over the rocks, but coming down was the hard part with no way to brace himself. Each day he went farther. Each day he grew stronger.

By the end of the week his whole personality had changed. He had been biting, sarcastic, bitter. He became mellow, gay and original. He was not fighting himself and the world any longer. He resigned from a routine job and applied for and got one as an office manager with more responsibility, less security, but greater future. He went to night school and finished his college degree. And he married. All this was the result of a week in the mountains when he put himself to the test of living up to his ultimate strength. As a result of his physical improvement, he developed a new personality, and, consequently, his whole life changed from the dead center of mediocrity to one in which he risked the challenge of a new business life and even a new personal life.

Like every other person, what you as someone with

a handicap want to do is live up to your own capacity. There is a saying that each man must carve his life from the block of wood he is given. What each of us can do is to carve his own wood, working its imperfections and brilliant swirls into the best possible design.

Loss of Job Crisis

It is difficult for anyone to lose a job, but it is especially difficult for a man. Although this chapter is addressed to a man and to a married one, most of it can be applied to single men and women. And much of it can be applied to those who were passed over for promotion or who failed to get an opportunity they wanted. There are many paths to a sense of defeat in one's work life.

A man who has lost a job naturally feels a great responsibility for his family, and also has a feeling of not fulfilling the male role as he should, that role which we build up so in today's world. It is all right for people to show their concern by saying, "Keep your chin up", or "Something will come along." These are sincere expressions of friends' interest, and they reflect exactly what you want, but they will come about only if you take the initiative to make them happen. Of course you are anxious — your way of life and your very self have been threatened. Although you may know that many others are going through the same experience, you have your wife and children to support, you have your bills to pay, and only you have to cope with your empty days and your frustration.

If you use the principles discussed in this chapter, you will learn something about your emotions and how they operate in your new status of being without a job. And too you will learn something about managing your emotions during a period of stress so that you come through the experience a whole and effective person.

1. In the first place everyone needs to have a complete and accurate picture of himself and of the world he lives in. This means that you must find out as much as you can about how you strike other people as an employee and as a person. You can get this only from the men to whom you have been responsible and whose judgment you trust. You need to know both your strong and your weak points. This means getting beyond the surface comments that appear in personnel folders and references. It means getting a wise evaluation of where you honestly stand — and such an evaluation will probably come from a superior who is a good enough friend to spend time in some long private sessions with you, in the office, after hours, on a fishing trip, perhaps at home over a beer, any place where people

can really talk. Such a man should be able to think in terms of you and your future rather than in terms of the organization you have just left. People like this are hard to find. Such a person can probably help you see losing a job as an opportunity to make some important discoveries about yourself on which you can build.

You will learn a lot during such sessions. You may find that it is not you but the organization that is found wanting: — over-expansion, too little work, taking a direction away from your specialty, to name a few. But then maybe you were let out and someone else kept. Perhaps this was because of seniority. Or the other man may have had strong personal contacts with your superiors Or he may have had certain professional or personal qualifications you do not have. Maybe your background was not versatile enough, or your work might have been as good as his, but the other man was more pleasant to be around. Here you are getting some place. Ask for specifics. You may have a distracting personal habit of cracking your knuckles. Or he may have shown he was better in an emergency and could take over while you tended to stick to the routine. Or perhaps he was there Monday mornings, and you — well, there were a few times you did not make it until later in the day. When it comes to a choice between hiring or firing two people, it is facts such as these that can make the difference if fundamental qualifications are the same.

Or maybe the job did not fit either your training or your ability. Everyone has a right spot, and the smart thing for you to do is find yours. The most miserable people I have ever seen were those who were doing something they did not like and, consequently, could not do well. They suffered daily torture. A successful career is one in which you do what you like and are paid for it. One of the real misfits is someone who is administering when he likes to do things himself, not lead others to do them. He may be department head when he likes to teach; office manager when what he wants to do is accounting; shop foreman when he would rather operate as an expert mechanic. There is supposed to be something especially good about leading so we see a scramble to the bandwagon, and the result is that there are too many candidates for chief when what is needed are more contented doers.

The thing to do is to get a picture of yourself and the business world of which you have been a part. It may be hard to take what you hear, but it is better to build your future on something that is real about yourself than on an idea that is only in your head. You need an accurate self-image. A well-known international industrialist told me he believed that every man should lose at least one job because nothing can force him into such a thorough and important evaluation of himself as taking stock to prepare to apply for a new one. You probably find it hard to see the wisdom of this when you are in the midst of the agony of being without work, but there is truth in it.

And there is another possibility in what you learn. You may hear about some positive characteristics that you never suspected — ones that you should take into consideration when looking for a new job. The point is to face the reality of who you are. As Robert Burns said, "Oh wad some power the giftie gie us, to see oursels as others see us."

2. How you take knowing exactly who you are is important. It is central to the way you operate now and through the rest of your life. Some people have very rigid images of themselves. They can only see themselves in one way, and anyone or anything that does not build up that self-image for them is rejected. Some people do not realize they are protecting a self-image at any cost, but that is exactly what they are doing if they say, "I didn't like that job anyhow," or "Everybody is losing jobs now. I can't help losing mine", or "I always knew the company wasn't fair to me." You know all the flattering excuses people can devise.

There are almost as many ways of facing the loss of a job as there are people. A very successful advertising man faced it realistically. He went home, told his wife about it, and said he figured it would take from three to six months to find another job. They had some savings, and together they figured how much a month that would give them to live. They cut expenses accordingly. Then he went to see or wrote everyone he knew. He worked, really worked at finding another job, using all his imagination and know-how. He broadcast to the world that he needed a job, applying, sometimes without introduction or appointment, at companies all over the western coast of the United States. After five months he found a job, one he has now been in fourteen years, one whose responsibilities he has expanded many times.

An older man, a small factory manager, was told he would not be needed after six months. He was hurt and ashamed and did not tell even his wife for two months. He was too embarrassed to let his friends know and so covered his situation by making it sound as though his work was fine — just fine. Finally, after several months of inward struggle, he confided in a friend who was president of an industrial plant. The friend offered him a position immediately. He could have been saved months of worry and self-doubt had he been realistic about facing his problem in the first place. The interesting thing about this man was that the experience gave him greater confidence in himself and his abilities. He had finally brought himself to see his self-image as that of someone who needed a job, and he found that it worked to be honest with himself. This gave him a greater sense of security and made it possible for him to allow his self-image to be even more flexible. He got himself through a difficult situation and grew in the process.

A young banker was asked to resign and was given a year's salary. He was so insecure that he had to maintain his self-image at all costs. He could not admit to himself that he was at fault. He turned his back on the world; it was wrong; he was not. Although he earned his living the rest of his life as a routine accountant, he never again trusted another person or allowed himself to grow dependent on anyone else. He had no home life. He had no friends. He lived entirely to himself, as a recluse.

These three men not only illustrate different ways of reacting to the loss of a job, but they also clearly illustrate the relationship between their sense of self and their inner security, and their approach to the problem.

I have known people who divorced wives, disinherited children, and refused clients — all to protect themselves from critical judgments and so preserve whatever image they had of themselves. Weak people will go to amazing extremes to preserve the image they have of themselves.

It is easy to see where people with such an urgent need to be right in their own eyes have gone wrong, but many others show milder degrees of this attitude. They must shade the truth in order to make life easier to take temporarily. A woman who was an accountant said that she lost a job the first time because she was a woman, the second because she was one of the last hired, and the third because she had red hair which the boss didn't like. But such frail comfort was short-lived. Her next setback was even harder to take because she had missed three chances to practice facing the truth. The truth was that her work was inaccurate and she was often late to the office. You can strengthen the ability to face the truth just as you can strengthen a muscle — by use.

3. Your next step will be the practical one of making every effort to get another job through whatever contacts are open to you. Agencies, unions, friends will give you ideas on openings. Sometimes people even create their own jobs by seeing something that needs to be done and developing it into a job. Or you may find that you could go back to school and get more training in a field related to your own work. And there is almost always commission

selling, if your abilities lie in that area. One vice-president in charge of sales for a well-known company said that *need* even more than native *ability* made successful salesmen — that a man could sell if he was hungry enough. (Of course, his product was not a technical one that required a specialized background.) Any job is better than no job. Some of the high-powered scientists who were released from government projects have driven taxis — not their line of work, but it brought in money until they could find something more suitable.

Any activity related to finding a job is constructive and worth putting time into: telephoning, filling applications, going for interviews. One idea or contact leads to another.

4. But eventually this may not take full-time and your days will be spent waiting to hear from the contacts you have made. You may discover this waiting really bothers you to the point of completely unnerving you. If this happens, find a good counselor and he can help you unravel the reasons. Counselors are expensive, but they do the important work of clearing up problems just the way doctors do when physical problems arise. You may find you have difficulties you were not aware of before you hit this snag of losing a job. The chances are you will not need to see a counselor, but each of us has his own range within which he can adjust, and this situation may be beyond yours.

5. Your personal life will be different. Every dimension

of your life will change. Your friends, at least most of them, are at work and that's where you used to make plans for poker, bowling, or tennis. Now these activities have very little part in your life because you are not around to plan an evening out. Then too you may not be able to afford them. If you have to wait very long to get work, you may find that some of the values of your life will change. At first, you may be reluctant to take the money the government, your company or insurance gives you, even though it is money that is due you for a time when you could be out of work. But you will probably find that the money you have to support your family is inadequate, grossly inadequate, to cover everything you have grown used to having.

But just as bad as not having enough money will be the new way of life you must get used to. There are no weekends. Every day will be a weekend day with no job to go to and no routine to carry you. If you own your own home, you are lucky, because then you may make improvements and many of them do not involve much money. You will not only have the satisfaction of making permanent investments in your home, but working hard and being tired are desirable at a time of distress. If you sit around and do nothing, you will be nervous and keyed up and hard for your family to live with.

6. The personal relationships you develop within your family at such times are important. Plan what they should be rather than just letting them happen.

You and your wife, strangely enough, can really have

quite an important experience together during this period, if you let her know how you feel and work out your problems with her. But if you keep how you feel to yourself, you will find something that happens in the family to take out your anger on and get mad about. And a merry time you will all have of it!

But you and your wife can get to know each other in a different way than you did during some of the better times you had together. Now the house and the work it requires can become a partnership. She can get away once in a while and you can do her work while she is gone. This gives variety for both of you. And you will appreciate, really appreciate, what your wife does because you will have walked in her shoes. A young wife with three children had to list her occupation on a health insurance application and she wrote she was a "live-in domestic." After a few all-day sessions of doing your wife's work you will see what this means.

There are many ways in which domestic work can be divided. I know a woman who teaches and her husband stays home and takes care of the children. They did not plan such a program. It worked out that way, and it seems to be an arrangement that works for them. But it might not be right for every couple.

Edna St. Vincent Millay's husband gave up a lucrative import business and devoted the rest of his life to maintaining the household and keeping distractions from her, publicly acknowledging to any and all that she deserved such a division of labor because of her superior qualities.

Make whatever adaptation of the idea of partnership

in the home you want to. But to do it, you, as a man, would have to be secure and strong, not weak. You would have to be secure enough to change your self-image to fit the situation instead of needing to maintain your male ego.

I called on a friend. Finally her husband came to the door, all six feet of him, apologizing because he hadn't answered sooner: "I'm not working right now so I was running the vacuum cleaner and didn't hear the bell." A less masculine and self-assured man would not have volunteered that he was doing housework. You yourself should come out of your present jobless situation a stronger and more flexible person, because you will have discovered your potential for adjustment and growth.

Get to know your children too. Play with them. Help them with their homework. You finally will have the time and energy to do projects they have long begged you to do. A university professor told me that his children knew his father in a way he never had — and that when he commented on this, his father said, "But I was earning a living in the years you were a boy, and I didn't have time to enjoy you as I'd like to. Now I'm not so busy and can know your children in a way I couldn't know you. Isn't that a sad thing to have to admit?" Now, much against your will, you are temporarily in the position of the grandfather with time to give your children, even though you may be without his peace of mind. If the children are old enough, they can find work, a more important step for them to take in making them self-sufficient than for them to have "everything money can buy."

If you change your self-image you can make this a good time of life that you and your family will never forget. "Guess who got dinner tonight? Will anyone help me clear up the mess I made in the kitchen? And you will be surprised at the recruits you get because your getting dinner is a novelty. You have also turned into someone real instead of someone who goes to a job somewhere all day and comes home at night tired.

Do not pretend that what has happened is not important. Think about it and talk about it. Of course do not go overboard because even your best friends will get tired of hearing about it. But do not bury how you feel. Sometimes in talking out a problem with a friend, the two of you find solutions you had not thought of alone, and it often clarifies the whole situation. In addition, talking helps get rid of your own pent-up emotion.

If someone drops in and thinks you are sick because you are at home in the middle of the morning, just say you are home because you are no longer with your old company but want — no, need another job and ask if he or she knows of anything. If your inclination is to murmur and avoid the issue, it obviously means you have not yet accepted the whole idea. This is not the way you like it, but it may be the way things are going to be for a while. Or perhaps your wife's family or your family can help in some way. After all, you would help them if they were in trouble. If you cannot see yourself letting them help you, you need to re-examine your self-image.

There are many possibilities and problems in losing a job. The suggestions made here are the applications of sound psychology to the situation you are in. But if you have been able to solve other problems, you will be able to solve this one. In the meantime you must maintain yourself and your family both financially and personally, so that you come out of this problem as a whole person and as part of a unified family group.

Life's Gradual,
Unspoken Disappointments

Between the ordinary changes in life and the crises discussed in previous chapters, there often lie major adjustments to circumstances which we seldom think of as tragic. Such adjustments are not drastic enough to rally the support of friends and family; they are the quiet, unspoken disappointments, the slow fading of hopes that served to motivate life.

Not every life can be triumphant, and some of the intangible but real disappointments often may be due to circumstances that could not be controlled. Some time ago I visited Mary, a middle-aged woman, who was in the hospital. She had never married and seemed settled into a life of material comfort with her parents to whom she was devoted. She was recovering from an exploratory operation for breast cancer, and I expected she would be happy and relieved at the negative diagnosis she had been given. She said she was grateful for that, but her eyes clouded with tears as she confessed in a low voice that she's hoped "to keep that part of me perfect, if I should ever marry." A whole lifetime of unfulfilled yearning was revealed in those few words, and many another woman has yearned with her. She was and is not alone in her quiet frustration. There are those women who are content without marriage, but most women who do not marry must, quietly and unobtrusively, change their life expectations.

An especially vulnerable spot for men is their business careers. In discussing a high school reunion, someone asked why Hal, who was so gay, so well-liked, had not come back. An old friend, as kindly as he could, told his friends about Hal's financial difficulties, of his slow inner defeat as he worked away at trying to make a living out of the drugstore his father had left him. He did not want to be in the drugstore business. When he could not sell it, he was stuck with a dead-end situation. Of course Hal did not want to go to the reunion in his one good suit. He would not have golf and trips to talk about with his old friends, and his image was not one he wanted to share with them. He would rather be remembered as he was in school.

Hal and Mary are tragic figures because they wanted to do more than they could. People who accept their own limitations cannot be in this sad position. It is the disappointment with one's self that hurts. We all see ourselves, not only as we are today, but as we will be in some tomorrow, and it is the picture that never comes true that creates gradual, unspoken disappointment.

There are also people who aspired to achieve in the arts and did not make it. They were the excited, creative ones with a fire that slowly died in the precarious business of trying to please the public. I never hear a professional orchestra without wondering which ones in it are thwarted soloists who did not make it in the gamble for success.

If you are in such a situation, the only solution is in accepting whatever it is that you cannot change and in enjoying to the fullest the satisfactions that are open to you. I know of very few people who have not had to do this to some extent.

Mary, for instance, found many areas of life to enjoy. She had very devoted friends. She held an important position of leadership in several organizations in the city she lived in. She became an authority on travel, so well-planned and executed were her trips. In short, she had a good life.

Hal, the unsuccessful druggist, finally found that he could arrange his time so that he had certain hours every day that he could use as he wanted to. He was a loved husband and father, and he spent those hours in activities that members of his family and he enjoyed. Their little sailboat and the public tennis courts carried them through the summer, with Scouts, church, and skiing in the winter. It was he who volunteered to help build the Scout camp, to take over as Superintendent of the Sunday School, to drive for the ski trips when his boys were in Junior High.

He graduated to being president of the congregation and chairman of the Scout Board when his sons went away to school.

Mary and Hal found they could accept who they were and the lives they led because they could change their image of themselves. And neither one made the mistake that some disappointed people do, the mistake of not daring to get excited about the future for fear of being hurt.

Almost all of us have made some private compromises which we have learned to live with, compromises through which part of us has not been fulfilled. The handicapped have learned to do this. All of us who make compromises must consciously compensate for them by develeoping interests that are satisfying enough to absorb the emotion we would have invested in the preferred way of life that never materialized.

Unfulfillment in life can be attributed to a variety of causes, many of them outside the individual, unseen and unsuspected. Recognizing causes cannot in itself magically change a life, but understanding those causes can help each of us learn how better to manage life.

CAUSES OF DISAPPOINTMENT

1. Modern society forces many of us to structure ourselves too specifically. We say to young people, "What are you going to be when you grow up?" "What are you training for?" The failure to achieve is not such an im-

portant part of primitive civilizations where people gradually grow through adolescence and into adulthood, quite naturally finding their place in the work of the village and family. A boy who could have done well in such a society may fail when he grows up in ours.

I often think of a plant I saw which had grown in a bottle. The plant grew bigger but it grew into the shape of the bottle. It can never be known what its shape would have been had it been allowed to develop naturally.

Other social influences that pull young people out of shape are too-great pressures to excel, boredom with routines in school or the armed services, the stulifying influence of repetitive jobs, and the too constant ready-made entertainment of television, radio and the movies. Surrounded by so many structured pressures, there is too little chance for a young life to know its own shape.

Moreover, we attach far too much value to certain kinds of work and to the supposed necessity for higher education. If work were harnessed to purpose and discipline and if financial success were not the only measure of success, there would be fewer people with a false sense of failure. If people could grow to be themselves, they would have little reason to feel themselves to be failures.

But there are many people who have broken through convention, people whose lives illustrate the importance of living rather than the importance of conforming to society's structure. A midwest industrialist had a serious illness that opened his eyes to what joy life could bring when removed from the constant pressure of business. After his illness he did not go back to his position, but instead changed to one in which he is virtually self-employed and has more leisure, less pressure, and greater flexibility of schedule. He and his family moved to a part of the country that is beautiful all year long, and they are thoroughly enjoying life there. He was perceptive enough to follow his inner needs and dared to radically change his style of living. Had he not been secure enough to follow his hunches, he would have gone back to his big job, in a big city, with big regrets. Too many men have stayed in work that did not suit them and so denied a part of themselves.

Otis Carney in his book *A New Lease on Life* tells of his change from a city to a ranch. You follow Mr. Carney and his family as each discovers a new sense of self — just as the plant might begin to spread out were it taken from the bottle. This is a present-day story of an important kind of personal success.

2. In addition to the problems that a modern society can create, parents sometimes unknowingly cripple the emotional growth of their children. This they do in several ways. They may impose their adult ideas and ambitions on them, thus giving a child a ready-made self-image that will not hold up well in the changes and pressures of life. For a girl, "Marry a nice young man and settle down." For a boy, "Of course, you'll study to be a doctor." Both of these are perfectly good plans if the young people develop them on their own. But these same plans are poor if parents impose them on young people because they reflect their own ideas of the good life and security for their

children, or because they represent their own thwarted ambitions.

Another way parents may damage their children's sense of self is to speed up their emotional growth and not honor their individual timing and unfolding. The late bloomers are forced into dating or parties when they would like to be playing dolls or collecting turtles.

And finally, some parents stunt their children's sense of self by offering too much help. I have seen a mother make a cake while leading her daughter to think she had made it herself. All the little girl actually did was to stay in the kitchen and say "Yes", when her mother asked, "Don't you think we'd better add the eggs now?" This kind of thing goes on a lot at Christmastime with toy trains and doll houses.

It is difficult to be a wise parent. In fact author Robert Hawkins feels that it is so difficult there should be classes in parenthood. In his article, "It's Time We Taught the Young To Be Good Parents", he not only recommends classes in high school on parenthood, but he also suggests that, "Because there is no practical way to identify inept parents in advance, it would be necessary to have a compulsory parent-training course that would reach virtually all potential parents."

As young people go from one period of life to another, they must grow emotionally in order to carry themselves through each successive stage. If their emotional growth does not keep pace there will be trouble, if not immediately, then later on. It is often in the late teenage years or in early adulthood that people crippled in their early emotional development begin to show obvious signs of distress. The teenager with stomach trouble, the young man who could not keep a job for more than a few months, the "perpetual student" who took course after course in graduate school to avoid facing the world, the young woman who at twenty-five was getting her third divorce — all of these people had a vague sense of disappointment with the way life had turned out. Each was trying to manage with a sense of self that had failed to develop properly. In such cases professional counseling is probably the best answer.

3. In addition to outside influences which deform individuals, there are inside influences in our natures that we often fail to take into consideration in building a life. If you observe your reactions, you can sense that you have two aspects to your nature. One demands security, stability, and regularity. The other is the part of you that craves risk, variety, and unpredictability. Each person has his individual combination of these characteristics. Some people demand something which stretches their capacities, something with an uncertain outcome — perhaps the great risk of being elected to public office or the lesser risk of being in a bowling tournament. Others have a temperament that responds to predictable work assignments, regular pay increases, and the security of a familiar place in which to work.

Harry, a brilliant young man, went to the University of California to get a Masters degree in marketing. His major professor, an international authority in his field, recognized Harry's ability and asked him to co-author a book rather than get a degree. But Harry had decided on a degree, a measurable and predictable objective. So he turned down the opportunity of an open-ended experience that would have given him new insights, contacts all over the world, and a vision that could lead to unknown opportunities. But Harry shied away from risk. It made him uncomfortable.

I was the Personnel Manager of a munitions factory during the Second World War. We employed many women, but I found it difficult to find female supervisors. Many women would not take a job that included the supervision of others, which can frequently be a disrupting experience, although accepting this responsibility would have increased their hourly rate of pay. These women knew themselves well enough to realize that the security of working on their own was more important to them than the risks of supervision and the additional money in their weekly paychecks.

But many people do not know themselves this well. They allow themselves to be lured beyond their depth into supervisory or executive positions that do not suit them. There is usually greater income connected with such a position and often more prestige, but, as I found out, a good machine operator, a good teacher, a fine salesman does not always make a good administrator. In addition to understanding the specific skill involved, an administrator has to have a combination of special characteristics, and the personal need for predictability and regularity are certainly not two of them.

On the other hand, some people want to deal with the unexpected and work in a variety of places. A young man looked forward to being a troubleshooter for a mechanical device installed in huge pieces of equipment that could not be brought to the factory for repair. The expertise of the factory, in the form of a young man, had to be taken to the device. He wanted to be out on his own.

Young women facing their first experience with keeping a home and raising children will quickly discover whether or not this new life provides the balance of risk and security that is comfortable for them. Some women settle happily into the work of domesticity and children. They find complete fulfillment within their own four walls. Other women love their homes and their families, but they also need an outside stimulus. Most such women, however, are in an income bracket that does not provide them with domestic help. Moreover, full-time jobs are often too demanding and part-time ones are scarce, routine, and too low paying to offset the cost of substitute childcare. *Catalyst*, a national, non-profit organization, has pioneered projects across the country to get women already educated, or those capable of being educated, back to work in jobs worth doing. The value of this organization is discussed in the book by Felice Schwartz and others and is listed in the bibliography. Fortunately Women's Lib has made many husbands more sympathetic to a wife's working.

And, of course, there are many people who have no choice but to stick to jobs that do not satisfy them. Numerous articles have appeared on the subject of the "blue

collar blues." Pay and benefits may be acceptable for the
unhappy workers, but no one can be paid enough for
working his days out in a job that curdles his soul with
monotony. In their article, "Collar Color Doesn't Count",
Stanley Seashore and Thad Barnave declare that "The
important factors that defeat workers are those that im-
pinge on the worker's self respect, his chance to perform
well in his work, his chance for personal achievement and
growth in competence, his chance to contribute something unique to his work — in short, his actualization."
But modern efficiency and cost accounting demand the
price of lives spent in routine in exchange for the thousands of items put on the market today for the public at
low cost.

If you are anchored to such a job, perhaps because of
your age or your family responsibilities, you must assess
your personal resources. It may be that you can use your
time off from your work in a program of training or education that will give you a chance at more interesting work
than you have now. It is sometimes the case that more
interesting work can develop from your current job situation, if you are fortunate. You keep yourself open to
new opportunities. But it is also possible that you might
have to make a compromise with life as consciously as the
handicapped do. You may have to take into account your
dead-end work as they take into account a handicap. Having truly assessed your situation you can deliberately plan
a new life in the time left over from your forty hours a
week at work, a life that adds the kind of variety and risk
you need. It is better to plan a program like this than to

smoulder and wait for something to happen that quite possibly may never materialize.

The important thing is for you to recognize the kind of person you are. People require different degrees of security and risk, and you must discover your own individual best combination. This combination is an intangible that is at the very center of building a life that fulfills you.

There are so many ways for a life to quietly and unobtrusively run amuck. In such cases no sudden tragic circumstance makes you take stock of yourself. But in a baffling and quiet way your day-to-day existence has not turned out to be what you imagined. With Gigi you seem to say, "There must be more to life than this!" We all can expect this feeling in certain stretches of life, but in all of it? No, not all of it if you obey the prime rule in solving problems: face reality.

Sometimes breaking your life down into areas and assessing the satisfactions and dissatisfactions in each one may help you see just how you are spending the most precious commodity, your time. Without the terrible emotional upheaval of a tragedy to nudge you to action, you may, on your own, have to analyze your problem and start a course of action that can help you climb out of the gradual unspoken disappointment you find yourself suffering.

A chance to live a life is the greatest gift you will ever have. If quiet dullness, a bewildering business, or a dredful feeling of being at cross-purposes with your experience engulf your days, that means that your weeks, your months, your years, your very life are in some way not right for you and the special kind of person you are. Reread this chapter, study it, mark it up, add new ideas, but make it your own as a guide in developing the kind of life that you could have within the framework of the limitations you must accept.

When Someone You Love
Goes Through a Crisis

One of life's most difficult situations is to stand on the sidelines while someone in your family, or someone close to you, experiences crisis. These crises are so individual that they cannot possibly be named. However, they can be grouped into general categories.

First there are people whose problems require your daily support — those who suffer a disability or long-term illness.

There are also those you love who have a problem with drugs or alcohol. Often such people do not consider that they have a problem, but you consider that they have one, one that can be solved only by a *change of attitude* on their part.

Third, there are *those who are not near you,* so that there is little you can do to help them actively. They may be in an institution such as a prison, a carekeeping school, or a psychiatric hospital. Or they may simply live far enough away so that you cannot give them direct and daily attention.

The range of personal tragedies is limitless. No one is immune from them. It has been said that if we could read the secret histories of men, we would find in each man's life deep sorrow and suffering.

Being the outsider puts you in an entirely different role from the one you play if the problem is your own. The whole object in facing a problem of your own is to wean yourself away emotionally from some aspect of your past life or your past self that you must learn to do without. As you begin to grow away from your past, your emotions are gradually freed to allow you to become involved with new interests and another way of life. For instance, in the death of someone close, you know that person will always be a part of your life in association and memory, but you know you must grow emotionally so that you are not upset whenever you are reminded of your former life together. However, you do not want such a release from active caring when you are helping someone you love who is in trouble.

CRISES REQUIRING DAILY SUPPORT

There are three general principles that you should keep in mind when faced with giving the best support to a loved one who is suffering a long-term debility or illness. These principles are essential in that they will help you avoid the mistakes which we are all too likely to make when caring for those we love.

1. You must encourage incapacitated persons to become as *self-sufficient* as possible. Regular physical checkups are, of course, essential, but, building on that base, the incapacitated person must be encouraged to plan his life around his strong points taking into consideration his limitations. Keep in mind, however, that limitations seem to reduce in direct proportion to desire. Read Harold Krentz's book, *To Race the Wind,* the story of how he, a blind boy, became a lawyer.

A young man with minimal brain damage lives with his family near a hospital, and for years he has delivered trays to the patients. He can work for short periods three times a day, he is always on call to replace absentees, and most important, he is well able to do this kind of work. His job not only gives him a schedule around which to build a day, it also gives him a good bank account around which to build a sense of security, and it develops his feeling of self-sufficiency.

Perhaps someone who is home-bound could build up an answering service. It would not only be a good business, it would also create an extension of interests.

It takes real ingenuity for people with a handicap to find work which gives them satisfaction. But a strong sense of self is the one capacity that overcomes obstacles which seem too high to scale.

2. If you are yourself comfortable about an incapacitated person, you will make others comfortable. Do not ignore the handicap but do not dwell on it.

A boy who spent his thirteen years of life on a portable table was introduced simply with, "This is our son Harry." He had been born with his handicap and never seemed to be aware that he was different from the other children who came in and out of his home engrossed in the activities they were all involved in. Someone born with a handicap has a different problem from a person who suffers a handicap through injury or disease. Such a person must have a strong sense of self to be able to change an already established image of himself. A high school girl, injured in a skiing accident, fought against using a wheelchair because she felt she looked more like her usual self if she was on crutches.

3. If you have been in constant attendance on someone ill or incapacitated, do not be surprised if both you and "the patient" need some change and relief from being together. Arranging for each of you to have involvements with a variety of people, interests, and activities is perhaps the greatest service you can give the person you are caring for.

A mother was nursing her high school son who had been injured in a hunting accident. But she saw to it that she was not his only companion. She planned his schedule so that his physical therapist, the young man who was his home-bound teacher, and the boy's friends brought into his life the variety of people and interests he needed to keep his spirits up in the days and months of his rehabilitation, the outcome of which could not be anticipated.

I have heard people say how selfless someone was who took care of another who was incapacitated. But I also remember the devoted wife who cared for nothing in the world so much as making her paralyzed husband comfortable and content. She used great imagination in planning their strangely happy days together.

CRISES THAT REQUIRE A CHANGE OF ATTITUDE

There are also those you love whose problems can be solved only by a change of attitude within them. It may be obvious to you that someone in your family should stop taking drugs, drinking or smoking, over-eating, but your opinion will generally have little influence.

Many rehabilitation centers for drug addicts and alcoholics operate on the idea that they cannot afford the time to work with people who do not themselves want to change. However, there are several ways people can be helped to change. Because such problems may be symptoms of some more fundamental problem, a doctor can determine if there is a physical basis for the symptom. If there is none, a psychiatrist can then determine if there is a psychological basis for the problem. If psychological problems are discovered, there is the hope that when the basic psychological problem is resolved, the symptoms will disappear.

However, all of this is much easier to write about than it is to put into practice. Usually people suffering from problems requiring a change of attitude do not want to change, and so do not want to go to either doctors or psychiatrists. They want to be left alone. Not every alcoholic or drug addict is saved. Skid rows are evidence of this, and smokers and fat people give obvious testimony to the persistence of their symptoms.

An important hope for the rehabilitation of people who resist change is the help given at organizations such as Alcoholics Anonymous, drug centers, and even Weight Watchers. Here the understanding of others who know the problem and have overcome it gives strong support in fostering change.

If all else fails, it is sometimes necessary to allow those who refuse to change to hit rock bottom in their lives in the hope that they may be jolted into changing. An example is the chiropractor who turned to alcohol to treat his disappointment in life. He had always been managed by his parents and was established in a business they set up for him. He did not do well in it and did not like either himself or his life, so he resorted to bragging to build himself up, even going back to his prowess on the football field in high school to find something of which he could be proud.

To help him face his unsatisfactory life and his own disappointment with himself, he gradually began to drink. His business failed and his wife finally divorced him. He made the rounds visiting their three children, and after several months, each one had to let him go on his way because he was so difficult to cope with when he was drinking. Having come to the end of his human resources, he stopped drinking. He had hit rock bottom. He unconsciously decided he would rather accept the person he was than continue as the drunk he had become. He took a job at a gas station, a job he would have previously thought "beneath" him. But he changed his self-image when he faced the reality of his own abilities and stopped trying to live up to the exaggerated abilities of the person his parents had built up. Having become whole, he and his wife were remarried, and they now live together with greater contentment than they had ever known.

His is an obvious case of someone who could not live a life based on a ready-made sense of self that had been imposed on him by his parents. It was not until he began to use his own honest sense of self as his basis for living that he could function as a whole person. If his wife had not divorced him, if any one of his children had accepted him as an alcoholic, he probably would not have changed. He would not have had to accept his real self.

However, allowing someone to hit rock bottom is a frightening gamble to take. There is great risk, but there is also the chance of great reward if a gamble such as this works out.

A husband who decides he wants to give up drinking must make that decision himself, but when he has, his wife can then do her part in helping change their way of life to back up that decision. In the first place she should not discuss the problem. She and her husband should find something besides a drink to look forward to at the usual

cocktail hour. They should go to parties after the cock-
tails but in time for dinner. They should find new interests that lead to new friends who do not drink. In carrying out such a program, she is giving support far more important than words. Of course this advice applies equally
to wives who have a drinking problem.

A problem closely related to alcoholism, and which
also requires a change of attitude, is drug addiction. The
same approaches apply to the possible solutions of both
of these problems with the exception that drug addiction,
in general, affects young people, many of whom are still
under the legal control of their parents.

There have been hours of debate by harassed parents
about whether to give financial support to children who
are of age but whose way of life the parents believe to be
degrading and dangerous. If parents subsidize such a way
of life, they may be preventing their child from sinking
to such despair that he eventually would change his life
himself. But if parents do not subsidize a child, they might
drive such a child to crime to support his drug habit.

The Drifters, by James Michener, includes the story
of a rebellious girl supported by a monthly check from
home. She lived all over Europe, became a heroin addict,
grew increasingly incompetent and finally died. She might
have come to the same end had her family not supported
her way of life. However she was never given the chance
to hit bottom. Her family, unwittingly, deprived her of
that potentially useful experience.

Control by the parents and accountability from the
minor children as the terms of adequate financial support

represent outward force that may temporarily take the place of the child's inner sense of responsibility that should have been built up over the years. Parents must decide for themselves the question of subsidization, knowing that their decision represents a gamble more than it does a reasoned choice, for there are no sure answers.

Or parents may secure institutional rehabilitation for their children. I know parents who sent their son to a school geared to helping problem boys, and it has paid off in terms of a son who is once more himself. However, on the son's return home, the parents had to have something to offer — a relationship with him that showed understanding and respect.

I told a friend about parents with five children who traveled Europe in a station wagon for four weeks without a single problem moment. My friend's immediate comment was, "Those parents have earned the respect of their children, or that couldn't happen." True enough, but the parents are not tyrants either. The respect the children have for them took years to build up by means of thousands of hours of real communication between the parents and the children. They have gradually let the children take more and more responsibility, which has resulted in a growing sense of self within each child. This provides a basis on which the children can make their own decisions. However, in rare and important situations, these parents do not hesitate to step in and take back some of the responsibility they have given and so help a child whose ability to make his own decisions has been mistakenly overestimated by the parents. It is feeding in responsibility, in the right amount at the right time, that builds a child's ability to take responsibility for himself.

Dr. Paul Goldhill has written an interesting book, *A Parents' Guide to Prevention and Control of Drug Abuse*. Half of this book is devoted, not to drugs, but to presenting the thesis that a good relationship between parents and child is the crux of preventing drug use.

One aspect of this idea is that an effective parent honors his child's right to have feelings. The other day I was visiting friends who have four children — superb ones! The youngest, a little girl of eight, had just come in from Christmas shopping for her family, and she was brimming with indignation at the fact that she did not have an allowance—that she had to earn her money by doing chores in the neighborhood. With her mother sitting right there, she told me her troubles. Her eyes snapped and her curls shook as she made her case with fervor and conviction, her voice strong with intensity. Whether the parents should or should not give her an allowance is not the point. The point is that she felt free to express her honest feelings before her mother — something much more important for her than having an allowance. The greatest assets which parents give children are not always tangible ones, and they are often not even measurable, except in the total quality of a life.

In dealing with drug abuse as in dealing with alcoholism we may do a disservice if we support the abuser either financially or emotionally in his weakness. However, once the person with the problem has decided to change, he needs all the help he can get from those who love him in creating a world encouraging to the new life he wants to make for himself.

WHEN YOU CANNOT BE NEARBY

Perhaps the most difficult kind of caring falls to the lot of those who must be separated from loved ones in crisis. The inevitable result of this situation is a terrible feeling of helplessness. You want so desperately to be *there*, doing whatever can be done, even if what can be done is very little. The families of Vietnam War prisoners suffered terribly in this respect, because they could not and did not want to free themselves emotionally from the husband, son, or brother who was lost to them, and yet their caring could not be expressed emotionally. Moreover, they were deprived of the healing process that finally brings peace of mind to the bereaved, the acceptance of final loss which must begin the healing process.

Others in a similar but less desperate situation await the release of loved ones from prisons or mental institutions. In such cases there is at least the security of knowing where your loved person is, and perhaps how long the wait must be.

But for all of you in a stand-by situation, your best life saver is to keep mentally occupied, emotionally involved, and physically tired enough to sleep at night. Most wives faced with the problem of waiting have worked or taken classes, and I know two of them who finished degrees. Getting degrees or developing skills is especially useful. This not only served to keep my two friends busy, but they felt it was a constructive step because it made them self-sufficient financially.

Your object is to use the time of waiting so that you as a person are able to help your loved one with the great adjustment problems he or she will face on returning to a regular life. Your life should not be allowed to deteriorate. You will have borne what you had to and grown to meet the problems. And whether you wanted it or not, your terrible experience of waiting will have helped you become a stronger person with a firmer foundation for living than you would have had without it.

You will certainly need to talk with close friends and others in your situation about your problems, for you need some kind of emotional release. A friend of mine told that on a trip to the West she stopped to see a woman whose husband was in a mental institution. She talked about the uncertainty of the husband's situation, the terrible strain the wife must be under and then about a beach picnic they had all gone on. Finally the wife had burst into tears. "It's so good to have you visit. My friends here won't mention Dick. You would think he had never lived. I know I can't make a nuisance of myself, but they simply ignore any reference I make to him. Shutting out my problem because it is unpleasant may help them, but it doesn't help me. It puts me in an unnatural, strained position with everyone I see in addition to the battle I have to fight constantly within myself."

People you know well often can help you by listening to you and not pointedly ignoring your problem. On the other hand, an obviously poor way to handle concern over such a problem is to share your trouble endlessly with anyone available.

A mother whose daughter had been in an institution for delinquents could talk of nothing else for months. Everything reminded her of her daughter and her own guilt, real or imagined. She monopolized the neighborhood coffees, spoiled bowling games and tyrannized at card tables with her discussions of her inward torture. Close friends spent time with her as she unburdened herself in private, and they were glad to do this. But she made her trouble the center of conversation for every group of which she was a part. Of course she was included less and less frequently as time went on. Finally she found herself treading water — at home alone.

People dig deep to produce the graves in which they bury themselves. Do not be one of those. Dig deep to keep yourself busy and growing during your stand-by period so that you are not consumed with futile worry. You cannot tell yourself not to worry. This does no good. You can, however, plan to do something that is absorbing enough to give yourself relief from your worry.

When someone you love is in crisis, you may suffer as keenly as though the problem were your own. In fact, sometimes you may wish you could shoulder the burden yourself. But the hard fact is that most tragedies must be borne by those who have suffered them. What you *can* do is conduct your life so as to have the strength to support your loved ones in their times of trouble.

When Someone You Love Is Dying

A young mother dying of leukemia and hospitalized for the last time said that her whole outlook was completely different from that of those around her. They spoke of things they were doing and their plans, for they could look ahead. But she had no future. She would not see her two-year-old daughter as a first grader or a bride. She would never have another summer, another Christmas, or another birthday. She would never leave the four walls of her hospital room alive. It was her world for the rest of her life. She was isolated from the concerns of ordinary life.

And yet for many years a conspiracy has surrounded

the patient who cannot get well, a conspiracy which makes the isolation of the dying more tragic than is necessary. "Don't let him know", people say. "Keep cheerful." But we say these things more to comfort ourselves. The approaching death of another is always threatening, for it makes each of us confront the fact of our own end. We, in our society, are not as realistic about facing death as people in many other cultures. Valid as the reasons may seem for the wall of illusion that the dying patient meets, it is cruel to isolate him at a time when he desperately needs honest human contact.

It has been found that almost every dying patient is aware that he is not going to live, and on his part he often keeps up a front of pretending he will get well to save his family. So in the last months of life the relationship between the patient and everyone he sees, doctors, nurses, minister, and family, is false. At a time of deep importance to him, at a time that should be filled with dignity, at a time in which he needs to share his thoughts and feelings, he must enter the cruel game that makes his total life one of sham and surface relationships.

Often a patient may share his grief over his own death with one other person, usually a professional counselor rather than a friend or member of his family. When he finally brings himself to talk to someone, he finds that he can more easily carry the burden of the fiction of his recovery which he feels he must maintain in order to help the others he must face.

However, there has slowly developed a more honest attitude toward death and dying. The subject has been discussed in magazine and newspaper articles and on TV programs by nurses, doctors and ministers. *Loss and Grief*, a book for the medical profession, has in it a whole section on how to deal with the dying patient. Panels, lectures, and workshops all over the country have begun to turn the tide against the well-meant deception and secrecy which surrounded "the dying patient" or "one with a terminal illness", those professional terms that hide the fact that someone deeply loved will not survive an illness.

Although patients seldom need to be told they are going to die, they do need to have someone listen to them and give them a chance to say what they are thinking — that they know they cannot get well. With very few exceptions, patients as they become aware of this, want to talk about it.

When someone you love is dying, you stand by helplessly grieving on the sidelines. A great responsibility rests on you as the one closest to the person you are losing, for you must decide what to tell him about his condition. Of course you will be greatly influenced by your doctor, but if you do not agree with him, you certainly have the right to discuss whatever point of view you have when the decision affects you and the patient you love so deeply.

Professional people who have had a great deal of experience with those who are not going to get well say they want three things; some hope, within the realm of possibility, in a treatment that will lengthen life, drugs that will reduce pain, and the assurance that others are going to stand by them as long as they are needed.

Dr. Elizabeth Kubler-Ross has been one of the people

largely responsible for a changed attitude toward the dying. She has talked with hundreds of people who were not going to live and has learned that most dying people go through various stages.

The first stage may be one of disbelief and denial when an individual is told how serious his illness is. This attitude may be maintained until the patient himself comes to terms with the idea that he is not going to live or until he feels that members of his family can accept it. If he feels they can, he is often relieved to drop pretense and face his death honestly with them. It is a relief too to be able to frankly take care of financial and personal arrangments that must be attended to, a will that must be made, or a child for whom he must provide.

When Eunice Tietjens, an author, was dying in Michael Reese Hospital, it was decided not to tell her she had cancer. She was a discerning woman and eventually suspected what the trouble was and pressed her doctor for answers. Finally, he told her the truth. "I wish you had told me weeks ago. I have much to write. If I had known I was dying of cancer, I would have worked harder at my writing", was her response.

A second stage is usually one of anger at the helplessness of being involved in a losing battle — one filled with pain, whose termination date is vague. During this time a patient is often cross with everyone — nurses who are not sufficiently attentive or are too attentive, family who come too often or not often enough. Such patients are imposing control over others, a control which they are helpless to impose over the changes in their own bodies.

And it is vital, energetic people who seem to irritate these patients most. Understanding these very natural reasons for a patient's anger makes it easier to respond to him when he is unreasonably demanding. We all have had an experience of an unspoken worry or irritation with something that we have taken out on someone or something else. The most obvious and hackneyed example is that of the man who is worried about business and therefore cross with his family. Professional people who work with the dying could be of great help to families if they explained to them this stage of seemingly unreasonable criticism and fault-finding.

Another stage that is often experienced is that of bargaining — usually with God — for more time in exchange for a promise, perhaps a life lived as a Christian in the future.

When this is not effective, the patient comes to a fourth stage where he faces separating himself from all that he has cared about. In mourning we suffer the loss of one person. A person who is dying must prepare himself to give up *all* the activities he has enjoyed and people he has loved. Never to see the full growth of the tree he planted last year or walk into his own home and garden again. Never to bowl another line; never to lead another business meeting. And he must relinquish *all* the people closest to him; never to see his son graduate from high school; never to know his grandchildren as teenagers; never to travel the country with his wife in his retirement. It is the relinquishing of all life that is so difficult, and there may very naturally be tears.

A great love story was acted out by an older man, a man much admired and greatly loved by the whole community in which he lived. His wife, a charming woman who still kept traces of the Gibson girl look of her youth, was a delight, but she was tortured by worry if anyone close to her had a problem. When having a physical examination, her husband found he had an inoperable cancer. When his illness became evident, he gave his wife another diagnosis for his illness and maintained a front for everyone involved. He kept to himself the grief he must have felt at giving up his whole vital life filled with challenge and warm friends and a loving family. He did this for his wife, bolstering her courage when she was discouraged about him. In spite of his depleted strength and constant pain, in spite of his own feelings, he did not let down once. After his death, his nurse gave a message to their only son. It was simply that his father had long known he could never get well.

Some people do not go through all the stages discussed. They may stop at the angry, rebellious period and never get beyond it. Or some may become dependent, almost like children in their need to have someone take care of them. Others may draw into themselves and not want to talk or respond. They seem ready to go although their physical life signs may still be good. Many patients want to talk about things that they have done, as though reviewing their lives And some, in their loneliness may need more than anything else to have people near them to talk to.

But most people, all through life and including this last period, want to live as fully as possible. They should continue living as normally as they are able; dressing, doing what they can for themselves and, if able, keeping busy with their usual activities such as seeing friends, reading, keeping up with the news, doing housework, writing notes, playing checkers or chess. A magnificent man, an actor, spent his last evening of life playing a two-handed card game, one he had played many times while waiting for his time to go on stage. We all know that a half hour spent involved in activity dissolves before we know it. But the same half hour spent in empty-handed and empty-hearted waiting seems endless. So activity geared to the capacity of each person is important.

Even more important is really communicating with a loved person who is dying. An architect told me that when he knew his wife could not live, he brought her home where they enjoyed the house they had developed and where they laughed and cried as they thought back over their life together. After she died, he said that he looked back on that time together as the greatest few weeks they had ever lived, so real and deep was their experience.

The stages of acceptance are not so evident or even so important to people whose basic emotional needs have been fully met at various periods of life. Such a person will come to the end feeling good about his life and about himself. The consideration of his death usually leads him to call upon the greatest personal resources he has built up in order to reintegrate his personality at a final high level of maturity. People want to make sense of the things that happen to them, and they especially want to make meaningful this last response to life's demands.

In *Lessons of History,* Will and Ariel Durant write,

"Life has inherent claim to eternity, whether in individuals or in states. Death is normal and if it comes in due
time, it is forgivable and useful, and the mature mind
will take no offense from its coming." Facing death is a
part of life and can be an important and meaningful part
of it if not denied.

But not all people die full of years, seasoned by time
yet diminished by a natural lessening of physical vitality.
Some must begin to face death when life has just begun.
Unless such young people are unusually mature, they
may be the ones who experience most acutely an adjustment in accepting death.

Dr. William Easson has found that young patients who
are dying have a variety of emotional reactions to death
depending on their age. Children under six usually have
no understanding of personal death. But grade school
children have what Dr. Easson calls a separation anxiety,
a natural need to be with those close to them. A child of
this age should, if possible, be allowed many visits from
family and friends and should not be left alone much.
Teenagers find it difficult to accept the idea of personal
death because it is a threat in their adolescent struggle
for independence. This conflict naturally creates a wide
variety of emotional reactions. Young adults, who are just
ready to begin their mature lives, may experience great
anger because death ends everything they have been working for.

One remarkable teenage boy did not follow the pattern
appropriate for his age. *In Death Be Not Proud,* John
Gunther tells of his dying son who maintained his interest

in life to the end. His father took him to the library just days before his death. Although his physical resources had long been nearly depleted, his superb spirit was unquenchable. His way of facing death reflected Dean Acheson's father's view of life. "What happened to you had to be borne, and how you bore it was more important than what it was—more important even than how it came out."

There are hospitals whose personnel are especially trained to take care of dying patients. The unit the staff works with is the patient and his family. Two such hospitals in the United States are Hospice, Inc., in New Haven, Connecticut and Calvary Hospital in The Bronx, New York. Another is St. Christopher's Hospice in Syndenham, England. These three institutions are staffed and programmed to make a last illness both meaningful and human.

An important question to consider is whether or not an individual has a right to choose his death. To be a person is more than to be vegetably alive. Euthanasia, or deliberately omitting to do something to preserve life, is increasingly resorted to when agreed upon by the patient, family, and doctor. Joseph Fletcher, in a *Harpers* article, as long ago as 1960 wrote, "Death control, like birth control, is a matter of human dignity. To perceive this is to grasp the notion widespread in medical circles that life is the highest good . . . The beauty and spiritual depth of human nature are what should be preserved and conserved in our value system, with the flesh the means rather than the end."

If you believe in what has come to be known as Death

with Dignity, signing a *Living Will* takes an important step toward participating in your own good death. It says, in part, that "If there is no reasonable expectation of my recovery . . . I request that I be allowed to die and not be kept alive by artificial means or heroic measures." A form for a *Living Will* can be obtained from the Euthanasia Educational Society listed in the bibliography.

In a discussion on what another person can do who is with a dying person, a nurse's aid said, "Because I am not a nurse, there seems to be nothing I can do, and I feel so helpless." The wise and compassionate doctor who was chairman of the discussion led her into seeing that she could be very helpful because of her concern and empathy. And he added quietly, "You see, my dear, there is nothing that any of us can do. Caring is the greatest gift anyone has to offer, and you can certainly give that."

Various attitudes reflect the way people feel when they come to the last stage — the stage where most people find they are ready to let go of life. Such a person may want one loved person who quietly helps care for him and who stands by in gentle physical contact, caressing his face or holding his hand. By this time, the patient has usually suffered such pain and physical change and has become so weak and listless that his death is a release from a condition no longer considered living. Giving him up as the person he had been was tragic. Giving him up as the shell he has become may not be so difficult.

But no matter how welcome the release from suffering, there is a finality about death that you are not prepared for, and you seek some universal understanding of which this experience can be a part. We do not know precisely how a human spirit comes into the universe with the birth of a baby. We simply know that it happens. The miracle in the evident reality of our entering life is locked in the mystery of the universe, and so it is with our leaving life. Both events are beyond our ken, both are profoundly moving as we face the miracle of a human being and the ultimate mystery of life itself.

Dealing With Grief

Someone you cannot live without is dead — yet you must go on living.

Grief is among the deepest pains that people endure. But it is one that nearly all of us experience in the course of a lifetime.

I knew grief when my husband died, and was forced to search deep and wide for an understanding of it. I can share with you what I found in that search for wisdom and of comfort, and what I have learned through counseling others.

Grief will finally run its course, little as you may believe that at first that can ever be. However, it will help you to know what happens to your emotions during grief so that you can use these emotions in ways that are helpful instead of ways that are damaging.

You will find that you go through three periods of experience in grief, each one blending into the next.

1. In the first sharp, emergency period you are of course shocked at being separated from someone who has been a vital part of your life. It is hard to make yourself realize that this has really happened to you. Early grief is usually so private that you do not know how other people have felt, and you may wonder at yourself, and your feelings, as you enter the unfamiliar world of grief.

You may blame doctors or nurses or even yourself for what has happened; you may be in a panic or have a sick, empty feeling inside yourself; you may not think or feel at all, and so for a short time not have to admit the death to yourself; you may feel tired, terribly tired; you may find it hard to sleep or eat; you may be completely disorganized and not know where to turn or what to do.

Perhaps you may feel you have nothing to live for, and temporarily this may be true. But eventually you will be involved in life again, although it will be a different life.

I know a service man whose son, an only child, was killed in an automobile accident. The thought of suicide tempted him. In order to prevent killing himself in a weak moment, he emptied his revolver of its shells and threw them into a lake. He did this because he knew that his suicide would then have to be planned and could not be a spur of the moment incident. He was wise enough to know that he did not really want to die.

Each major religion has a special comfort to offer at a time of death. Consequently, your best human support may be from a friend of your faith, either a close personal friend or a leader in your own religious institution who can help you interpret your loss in the light of your special beliefs.

Sometimes, when death follows a long illness, grief has to some extent already worked itself out. Then the actual death may not be such a shock. After a wasting and painful illness, there may even be a sense of gratitude that there will be no more suffering.

One thing that sometimes makes first grief even harder than it need be is that some people — especially men — have an idea they should not cry. But you who grieve have a real need to release damaging emotions by crying. There are times, many of them, when there is nothing else you can do. But there are other times when you may choke back tears when you should let them flow in order to release tension.

I have called on people who had just lost someone close to them, and they apologized when tears came to their eyes. But crying is natural at such a time. Not only that, it is healthy.

I went to a funeral not long ago. It was for a truly magnificent man who died in his late forties. His wife had died just seven months earlier. During the service, his daughter hastily wiped a few tears away, from time to time. But why shouldn't she cry? Why shouldn't she indeed?

There is no particular pattern which you should follow during the days before the funeral. If others want to do something for you, let them. It does help to have people in your home who can answer the telephone and doorbell because there will certainly be times when you are not able to or will not want to. If seeing people who come to call gives you comfort, see them. If you want to be by yourself or with a relative or close friend, do that. Others can meet the friends who call. Do what helps you most and seems most natural to you as each day unfolds.

What those of us in grief usually need is temporary support and love to replace that given by the person lost. We need such support until we gradually grow able to go on alone.

The wisdom of the Jewish rituals of mourning takes into consideration this void in the lives of those newly bereaved. During the week following the funeral, the family stays at home, and friends come to visit. They all sit together and talk of the person who has died, remembering, perhaps crying, at last even laughing over something that was said or done. The families get great comfort from these days and evenings because they know that others are grieving with them over their loss.

Of course, some people might not like such a custom at all. It is true that we in grief may be different in our ways of meeting the problem, but we are alike in that we must eventually learn to handle our emotions so that we resolve grief and again become whole people.

People in first grief often experience unexpected emotions. One of them is *guilt*. It may be specific guilt over not having had an extra nurse or having failed to call the doctor sooner. Or it may be a vague kind of guilt whose source cannot be identified. Vague guilt may be caused by an unconscious resentment growing out of the limitations imposed by any close relationship. "How I'd love to go to that meeting. But I can't because, of course, there's the baby, or my husband's dinner to get, or my mother's day to spend the afternoon here." These fleeting, natural, feelings may, after a death, develop into a general and indefinite guilt. Another unexpected emotion which you may experience is anxiety, anxiety over an unstructured future. And you may feel *anger* at what has happened to you and your life. But as you grow beyond your first grief, these strange emotions begin to disappear.

Finally the flowers given you fade and the dishes are returned, dishes that brought food for the bereaved, that strange, new person you have become. Callers are less frequent, and you are faced with days, weeks, months, and years of a new life.

2. By now you have moved into a second period devoted to the long, slow process of resolving your grief through "grief work." This involves dwelling on your problem *mentally* as much and as long as you need to. You cannot help but *think* about the person you have lost and all the problems you face in adjusting to a new life that you dread.

You may also want to *talk* about your problem. You were probably used to talking things over with the person you have lost, and it is very natural that you should want to continue to do this with sympathetic members of your family and with friends.

You *think* and *talk* about how you feel in order to very gradually break the emotional ties to the person you have lost. This does not mean that you can ever forget that person. It simply means that you can eventually think or talk about the one you have lost and not be emotionally upset. You will not be upset because, almost without knowing it, you will have very gradually shifted your emotions from your grief to other interests in life.

When you are absorbed in grief you are like someone in severe physical pain. Such a person cannot pay attention to anything but the pain, and for him healing will be a physical process. Your deep mental pain will be relieved by an emotional healing that results from facing your loss and letting grief run its course; that is, by doing "grief work."

The work of breaking the ties to the hundreds of associations you have built up takes months or perhaps a year or more. You will be continually wounded by incidents and expressions that no one else would understand. One woman told me that she could never again linger over a second cup of morning coffee, because this was the time of day when she and her husband talked together after the children had gone to school.

If you have lost a son it will be devastating to see boys all dressed in their oversized baseball suits running off to Little League. Or you may almost start with guilt at twelve and four and eight when you realize you are not giving your father his medicine, your father who will not need medicine again. A high school girl admitted that dressing for school was the hardest time of day for her because she and her sister, just a year older, had always exchanged clothes and pieced together their outfits from both their closets as they got ready for school. Her sister died, and now she dresses quietly alone. The nicknames—they are almost the hardest to bear. For one man, packing for a trip was especially difficult since his wife had always done this for him. For married people "our" and "we" are words that no longer are used except when talking of the past. The changes are endless and entirely personal. Your despair, cruel as it is, is a sign that your grief is following the usual pattern. It means you have accepted the death and are trying to make an adjustment to what it means in your life.

Slowly feel your way back to life. You need outside experiences, but if these experiences intrude too soon, they are only distractions which interfere with your vital "grief work."

A neighbor whose mother had just died came to have supper with me some years ago. We had planned that she could come and leave as soon as she wanted to. But even in the short time she was with me, I could see there were moments when she lost contact with the outside world and faded into herself. Her conversation drifted and she stared into space. Still, it was good for her to come and try herself out in a quiet, short experience with only one person, good for her to be able to act as she felt and not try to keep up a false front.

However, as comforting as seclusion and understanding friends may be, you must not allow either to become a permanent crutch. Even though you feel you can never wean yourself from your past life, a beginning must be made.

You know that when you *want* to do something, it is easy. But when you *determine* to do something, you must force yourself. When you are in grief, everything is forced at first. But when emotion takes over, even for a moment, and you do something because you *want* to, your healing has begun.

Go back and re-read pages 29 through 32 in the chapter YOUR OWN TRAGIC LIFE CHANGES. This is a simple illustration of how I began to change from determining to do thing to *wanting* to do them.

There can be no hurrying this process. A comparison is the lifting of a scab. When it is ready to come off, it lifts easily. If it is torn away too soon, it tears the flesh and healing is prolonged. And so it is with the emotions of one who grieves — they cannot be pushed too fast.

Shifting your emotions from your grief to other interests is so painful, it is amazing that this pain in the lives of people going through "grief work" is taken so much for granted by others.

Two things that are very important to you during this second period: the continued need to cry and the help of friends.

The Need to Cry — As time passes. you may try to control your emotions and behave as you believe a disciplined person should. But you will still find that "a good cry" actually makes you feel better. It is wise to allow yourself to cry when you are alone. Empty yourself of your pent-up emotions, and then you will not be likely to cry when you are in public and are caught unaware by some unexpected reminder — a song or someone ahead of you on the street who, by a walk or the tilt of a head, reminds you of the one you never again will see.

An older man whose son was killed in the war kept up as men and boys think they are supposed to do. He dammed up his emotions within himself. Weeks after the funeral he finally broke down and cried without control. After that "good cry" his healing began.

After his daughter died in a skiing accident, a doctor told me that every morning he went to the basement and "bawled" where his wife could not hear him. He said "I just don't think I could have gotten through the first weeks if I hadn't done that."

Gradually you will find that you need to cry less often as you begin to get back into life again. But do not be surprised, especially if tears come to your eyes easily, to have them well up at some unexpected reminder or some private memory of the person you have lost.

The Help of Friends — Other people do not mean to be cruel or even indifferent, but they are often embarrassed by those of us in grief. After they have sent flowers or a card, brought a cake or donated money to a memorial and gone to the funeral, they feel they have done what they can. They have accepted the death and expect that soon you will accept it too.

I have heard so many people in grief say that late afternoons and Sundays are the hardest times to get through because that is when families are together. These times are especially difficult if you are left alone by a death. You never had to plan anything special to do because there was always your brother, husband, wife, or friend who could be called at the last moment and to do whatever you felt like doing. But being alone is different. These are the times when friends can help by asking you to come for a simple supper or to join them for a movie.

The greatest help of all is knowing people you can go to at any time when you desperately need companionship and understanding. However, you do not feel like following up a "come-any-time" invitation unless you have been asked to that home so many times that you know you are part of the family and welcome. Often family members do not live near each other as they used to, and good friends can fill this natural need for family closeness and informality.

You may not believe it, but the way your friends feel and act can hinder "grief work." If friends give you the impression that they want you to act just like your old self again, you may be tempted to cut short your "grief work" and try to adjust to what they expect.

But do not allow yourself to be hurried. You *must* suffer through grief because active suffering is the bridge to your healing. Studies have shown that grief which is not resolved may cause physical difficulties or emotional problems.

There was a time when bereaved people were given more helpful support from society than they are today. This sustaining and natural support came from three institutions:

1. The family which tended to remain in or near one community.

2. The church around which people's lives largely centered.

3. The year of mourning which was generally practiced.

Today, the influence on the bereaved of all three of these institutions has been gradually reduced, and the bereaved now find themselves in a society much less aware of their needs. The bereaved themselves do not necessarily know how best to handle their new emotions. This is the reason that there is a need to give both the bereaved and society help in understanding the emotional experiences which were once a more natural and a more real part of life than they are today.

Geoffrey Gorer did a survey of fifteen hundred bereaved people in England. He found that often people in grief are not given the help they need from others. The survey showed that, too often, people are treated as though grief were "a weakness instead of a psychological necessity."

Do not be tempted to avoid grief with sleeping pills, drugs or alcohol. You cannot drown sorrow. Nor can you run away from it by going out a lot, a less obvious way of by-passing "grief work."

If you do not feel like yourself again in a year or two, go to see someone who can help you, perhaps your minister or doctor; one of them may suggest a counselor who can give some special advice that can help you. Remember that the most important consideration at this point is your "grief work." Do whatever gives you the greatest help in gradually working through it.

As you resolve your grief you come into the third and last period when you pick up life again. You will find that there is no sharp break between these last two periods, but rather a gradual decrease in emphasis on grief work and an increasing emphasis on your present life. In building a new life, you may continue with an interest you have always had or you may discover something new. But whatever your interests, you must really care about them enough to gladly invest your time and your emotion.

A woman who lost a brother with whom she made her home spent almost full-time as a volunteer doing social work in the nursing home where he had spent the last months of his life. Through a special organization, a retired lawyer whose wife died gave his knowledge of a lifetime to people who needed legal help but did not have the money to pay for it. I know of others who have promoted a community garden project, given quilting instruction, or provided free babysitting for the neighbors. These people found that giving themselves away was the path to finding themselves again — finding themselves at peace with their memories.

You may have major practical decisions to make, decisions such as selling your home or moving to another community. Unless for financial or other reasons you have to make such changes soon after the funeral, wait until this last period. You will know when you are ready to make major decisions as surely as a baby's body knows when it is ready to walk. You will be ready emotionally to take important steps because you will be sure within yourself what you want to do. The decisions will almost make themselves. Soon after my husband's death, I would have felt lost had I sold our home. But later, without making a conscious decision, I walked up to a real estate man at a meeting and put the house on the market. I do not pretend to know what happened within me that made this possible. I merely offer it as an example of what I mean by being "ready emotionally" that develops in this last period.

There is an unconscious pull toward life that is a help to people who grieve. People have a great ability to move forward, an ability which has been called "the main spring of life." It helps them reach out toward life as surely as plants turn toward light. It is this miraculous inner pull, coupled with the support of your religion, family, and friends which will help you rebuild your life. If you resist grief, it can destroy you and the years of life remaining to you. But if you accept your loss and allow grief to follow its natural course, you will achieve the rebirth and growth of grief's slow wisdom.

Conclusion

Never morning wore to evening,
but some heart did break.

In Memoriam — TENNYSON

Between one morning and one evening, the kind of tragedy that happens to others came to you. The core of your
existence was threatened by a death, a divorce, a drastic
physical change, and your chief defense in living through
that tragedy was the strength of your sense of self. Weak
or strong as that sense of self was, it was your best support
in managing a personal crisis.

If you allowed yourself to suffer the full reality of your tragedy, if you did not camouflage it with false hope or dull it with drink or drugs, you have found a reserve power within yourself which, through some miracle unknown to man, gave you the strength to suffer what came to you.

You have absorbed other changes in your life and resolved other griefs, and these prepared you for a tragedy that forced new growth on you — new growth that helped you reach a level of personal strength you had never known before.

In this experience you learned a wisdom that has been discovered and rediscovered independently through the years by new generations of those who suffered. A message in "Desiderata" from Old St. Paul's Church of Baltimore said, "Nurture strength of spirit to shield you in sudden misfortune." Nietzsche reflected this idea when he said, "A strong and well constituted man digests his experience just as he digests his meats, even when he has some tough morsels to swallow."

This strengthening of the sense of self is the prime task of each life. Its growing, its becoming, continue through every year right up to the end. And this strength, which constitutes your greatest achievement, is the indispensable cornerstone for the other accomplishments and relationships which give meaning and dignity to a life.

Bibliography

Callaway, Helen B. "Change Linked to Illness." *Dallas Morning News.* Dec. 20, 1972.

Carney, Otis. *A New Lease on Life.* New York: Random House, 1971.

Clifton, Bernice. *None So Blind.* Chicago: Rand McNally & Company, 1962.

Easson, William M., M.D. *The Journal of the American Medical Association.* (July 22, 1968) : 203–7.

Elliott, Grace Loucks. *To Come Full Circle Toward an Understanding of Death.* Privately printed, 1971.

Euthanasia Educational Society, The. 250 W. 57th St., New York City, N.Y.

Fisher, Gary. "Psychotherapy for the Dying: Principles and Illustrative Cases." *Omega* vol. 1: no. 1 (February, 1970) , 3–17.

Fletcher, Joseph. "The Patient's Right To Die." *Harpers* Magazine, October, 1960.

Frankl, Viktor. *Man's Search for Meaning.* New York: Washington Square Press, 1969.

Fraries, Gloria M. "Cancer, The Emotional Component." *American Journal of Nursing* vol. 69: no. 8 (August, 1969), 1677–81.

Gardner, Richard A. *The Boys and Girls Book About Divorce.* New York: Benton Books, 1970.

Goer, Geoffrey. *Death, Grief and Mourning.* Garden City, N.Y.: Doubleday and Company, 1965.

Goldhill, Paul M. "A Parent's Guide to the Prevention and Control of Drug Use."

Gordon, Ernest. *Through the Valley of the Kwai.* New York: Harper & Row, 1962.

Gunther, John. *Death Be Not Proud.* New York: Harver, 1949.

Hawkins, Robert P. "It's Time We Taught the Young How To Be Good Parents." *Psychology To-Day,* November, 1972.

Hudson, Carol Burdick. "Negative Number" — Unpublished poem.

Hunt, Morton M. *The World of the Formerly Married.* New York: McGraw Hill Book Company, 1966.

Kastenbaum, Robert. *The Psychology of Death.* New York: Springer, 1970.

Kazantsakis, Nikos. *Zorba the Greek.* New York: Ballantine Books, 1953.

Krentz, Harold. *To Race the Wind.* New York: Putnam and Sons, 1972.

Kubler-Ross, Elizabeth. *On Death and Dying.* New York: Macmillan Company, 1969.

Lederer, William, and Jackson, Don D. *The Mirages of Marriage.* New York: W. W. Norton & Company, 1968.

May, Rollo. *Love and Will.* New York: Norton and Company, 1969.

————. *Man's Search for Himself.* New York: W. W. Norton & Company, 1953.

Morris, Sarah. *Grief and How To Live With It.* New York: Grosset and Dunlap, 1972.

Mutze, J. *Bereavement.* London: Butterworth Press, 1971.

O'Neill, Vera and George. *Open Marriage.* New York: M. Evans and Company, 1972.

Ruch, Floyd L., and Zimbardo, Philip G. *Psychology and Life.* Glenview, Illinois: Scott, Foresman and Co., 1971.

Rusk, Howard. *A World To Care For.* New York: Random House, 1972.

Schoenberg, Bernard and others. *Loss and Grief — Psychological Management in Medical Practice.* New York: Columbia University Press, 1970.

Schwartz, Felice N. and others. *How To Go To Work When Your Husband Is Against It, Your Children Aren't Old Enough, and There's Nothing You Can Do Anyhow.* New York: Simon and Schuster, 1972.

Seashore, Stanley E., and Barnave, J. Thad. "Collar Color Doesn't Count." *Psychology To-Day,* August, 1972.

Skinner, B. F. *Beyond Freedom and Dignity.* New York: Knopf, 1971.

Toffler, Alvin. *Future Shock.* New York: Random House, 1970.